D0214298

NATIVE AMERICANS

Interdisciplinary Perspectives

edited by

JOHN R. WUNDER
CYNTHIA WILLIS ESQUEDA
University of Nebraska-Lincoln

A GARLAND SERIES

NATIVE AMERICAN PEDAGOGY AND COGNITIVE-BASED MATHEMATICS INSTRUCTION

JUDITH E. HANKES

GARLAND PUBLISHING, INC.
A MEMBER OF THE TAYLOR & FRANCIS GROUP
NEW YORK & LONDON / 1998

Copyright © 1998 Judith E. Hankes
All rights reserved

Library of Congress Cataloging-in-Publication Data

Hankes, Judith E.
Native American pedagogy and cognitive-based mathematics instruction / Judith E. Hankes.
p. cm. — (Native Americans)
"Describes a Ph.D. dissertation study completed in 1994 at the Oneida National Elementary School in Oneida, Wisconsin"—Introd.
Includes bibliographical references and index.
ISBN 0-8153-3113-4 (alk. paper)
1. Oneida children—Education (Preschool)—Wisconsin—Oneida County. 2. Mathematics—Study and teaching (Preschool)—Wisconsin—Oneida County. 3. Oneida philosophy—Wisconsin—Oneida County. 4. Oneida Indians—Social life and customs. 5. Cognitive styles in children—Wisconsin—Oneida County. 6. Cognition and culture—Oneida County. I. Title. II. Series: Native Americans (Garland Publishing, Inc.)
E99.O45H35 1998
372.7'01'9—dc21

98-44968

Printed on acid-free, 250-year-life paper
Manufactured in the United States of America

Contents

Introduction

This book describes a Ph.D. dissertation study completed in 1994 at the Oneida Nation Elementary School in Oneida, Wisconsin. The study compares traditional Native American pedagogy with that of Cognitively Guided Instruction (CGI) and investigates the influence of CGI on the mathematical problem solving ability of Oneida Indian kindergarten children.

The first step in completing the study was to identify the methods of instruction common in Native American teaching. Having proposed that there is a generalized Native way of teaching, it is important to recognize that Native Americans represent more than 300 different tribes (Butterfield 1963; Stuck in the Horizon 1989) and that each tribal group possesses varying linguistic, cultural, social, political and economic dimensions. Consideration of such diversity forces one to be cautious when overgeneralizing across tribes (Brasswood & Szaraniec 1983), however, many studies point out that there are notable consistencies among Native peoples (Tharp & Yamauchi 1994; Cahape & Howley 1992; Indian Nations at Risk Task Force 1992). Specifically informal and formal teaching practices, shared by Native American teachers across tribes. These practices comprise what is referred to within this study as Native American pedagogy.

The second step of the study was determining whether the generalized Native American pedagogy corresponded with traditional Oneida instruction. This involved interviewing five educators from the Oneida community. An important realization evolved out of this process—the Oneida educators had not considered what a Native American way of teaching might be and whether Oneida instruction would correspond with that way. This realization prompted an investigation into the cultural values that informed communication patterns within a traditional Oneida classroom.

Determination of whether Native American pedagogy and Cognitively Guided Instruction were compatible was dependent upon one teacher's knowledge of both approaches: an Oneida kindergarten teacher, after participating in two thirty-hour CGI workshops, implemented the approach in her classroom. This teacher, having reflected on how Oneida culture values influenced her teaching and how her teaching corresponded with Native American methods, identified the commonalties between Oneida/Native American pedagogy and Cognitively Guided Instruction as she understood them.

The final stage of the study involved documenting the mathematical problem-solving ability of Oneida kindergartners taught with Cognitively Guided Instruction.

Three research themes focused the study: first, determining the impact of Oneida culture values on traditional Oneida instruction and the relationship of those values to a generalized Indian way of teaching or Native American pedagogy; second, determining an Oneida kindergarten teacher's views regarding the cultural compatibility of Cognitively Guided Instruction; and third, determining the problem solving ability of Oneida kindergarten students taught with Cognitively Guided Instruction. Three research questions facilitated the investigation of these themes:

1. What cultural values influence Oneida instruction, and do those values correspond with the values, which underlie Native American pedagogy as outlined in the literature review?
2. Did the participating kindergarten teacher believe that Cognitively Guided Instruction is a culturally compatible way of teaching mathematics to Oneida/Native American children? If so, why?
3. How did Cognitively Guided Instruction influence the mathematical problem solving ability of the Oneida kindergarten students in this study?

The Researcher's Paradigm

A paradigm is a world view, a general perspective, and a way of breaking down the complexity of the real world. As such, paradigms are deeply imbedded in the socialization of adherents and practitioners, telling them what is important, what is reasonable. (Patton 1975, 9)

Discourses can never be neutral or value-free; discourses always reflect ideologies—systems of values, beliefs, and social practices. (Fairclough 1989; Foucoult 1972; Gee 1990)

Recognizing that paradigms are socially constructed and that discourses are subjective, informed by the lived experiences of each speaker or writer, it is important that I provide information about myself to enable the reader to better understand and assess the ideas, findings, and proposals advanced within this study.

Foremost, I must situate myself as a creationist, a believer in a Higher Power. Related to this belief is my cognitive constructivist view of the learner, a view that recognizes the cognitive capabilities and neurological likenesses of all humans (Fosnot 1989; Gardner 1985; Magoon 1977; Von Glaserfield 1989). But then, I am also a social constructionist, an individual who believes that though humans are cognitively more alike than unalike, lived experiences and social interactions determine who we are and what we value (Gergen 1985; Shotter 1993; Vygotsky 1978, 1986, 1987; Wertch 1984, 1985). Finally, I identify myself as an ethical pragmatist, one who values equity and works pragmatically to achieve it.

Cognitive constructivist, social constructionist, ethical pragmatist, labels discursively produced by academics, situates me as an academician. However, prior to acquiring the meaning of such labels and achieving such status, a life rich with varied social interactions produced the personal values, which underscore these labels. In order to understand why I elect to claim such values, you must know about my life. So, I have chosen to include a short personal narrative. The narrative relates specifically to mathematics and provides insight into why I elected to investigate culturally compatible mathematics instruction for Native American children.

A Personal Narrative

I avoided mathematics courses in high school, choosing only to take the basics—general and consumer mathematics. Because of high science placement tests scores, I ended up being tracked into chemistry and physics. However, having been told by a counselor that I lacked the mathematics necessary to do well in these classes, I obliged him and self-fulfilled the prophecy by barely maintaining passing grades. It wasn't that I struggled with the content, I simply reconciled myself to the belief that these were mathematics courses, and since I couldn't do math, I couldn't do chemistry and physics as well. I remember perplexed teachers assuring me that I would do fine if I just applied myself. I shrugged their encouragement off, rarely opened the texts, and clowned my way through class sessions. It is a fact that fear of mathematics greatly influenced my general underachievement during high school.

Why did I feel as I did about mathematics? What was it about my childhood that led me to first devalue mathematics, as I'm certain that I did, and later to think of myself as mathematically incompetent?

My family was very poor, economically at the bottom of the poverty scale. Mama and Papa homesteaded a small island fifteen years before my birth, and on this island reared five children. I was the youngest. In the summer, Papa worked odd jobs, and during the winter he trapped. Mama didn't work a paid job, but she worked—carrying drinking water, washing clothes by hand, and gardening.

Domestic violence and neglect had limited my father's education to finishing fourth grade. He had been born on the Ojbwe St. Croix Reservation in Wisconsin. After his mother's death he was taken to an orphanage near Chicago and was eventually adopted by a cruel woman. When he was ten, Papa ran away and lived on the streets of Chicago until he moved, at the age of nineteen, to what was to become our island home. Mama was Swedish and also an abused orphan. She escaped her abuse by marrying Papa at sixteen and moving to the island.

What does this have to do with my low math achievement? It has everything to do with it. I remember watching Papa struggle to complete computations and then seeing him hand the paper to Mama saying, "Ruth, check it." From early on, I knew that Mama was better at math than Papa—she knew her time's tables and long division. The problem was, Mama believed that she was mathematically incompetent. However, she and Papa each valued reading. Evenings were spent reading books aloud, and Mama loved to write. But, I do not remember Mama or Papa ever talking positively about mathematics, ever flashing a flash card, or ever posing a math problem to be solved merely for practice.

It wasn't that my childhood was entirely void of mathematics. My brothers and I were financial entrepreneurs. We speared carp and sold them to the old black men fishing across from our island. We caught worms, crabs, and hellgrammites and sold them for bait at a gas station, we planted seeds and sold the flowers, baked cookies and sold them door to door.

For young children, our arithmetic skills were incredible. We learned very early how to make an honest profit from an investment; Mama and Papa taught us to be honest, never to steal, never to accept charity, and to share whatever we had. Materialistic poverty taught us to be self-sufficient problem-solvers.

Our rich situated learning experiences should have prepared us to become successful mathematicians. However, something broke down and that something was our formal education. Being labeled "river rats" and "half-breed trash", prompted my older sister and two brothers to drop out of high school. My youngest brother, and I graduated, but my graduation seemed to have happened to me, as though I had nothing to do with it. I preferred to stay home rather than go to school. I preferred wading the river, searching for bird's nests, sitting and drawing, helping Mama garden and cook. School was a place where I had to be tough, ready to fight when someone teased. I remember my brother being pantsed on the playground by a group of kids who had bet that we were too poor to buy underpants. I grabbed a baseball bat and swung it violently at the boys who were pulling at his trouser legs. I was not going to let them learn that they were right.

No, I was never part of the system, and mathematics wasn't important to me because the system wasn't important. Even now, as I write these words, deep down, I feel the same. I feel that I understand how lived experiences impact on mathematics performance, specifically, how the culture of materialist poverty impacts on mathematics performance. More often than not, today's children of poverty have parents, like mine, who have been alienated from the system, and their alienation influences the level of mathematics assistance and support they care about giving or are capable of giving. They are not inferior parents, and their children are not cognitively inferior. It's just that their lived experiences differ drastically from those of middle class parents with socialized beliefs of manifest destiny and conspicuous consumption, middle class parents whose social status avails opportunities to pursue a consumptious destiny.

Labeling and Political Correctness

Five hundred years ago Christopher Columbus came to America and mistakenly called the indigenous people Indians. The name stuck. The voyager's error is recognized in the term American Indians. More recently a move to replace both designations with Native Americans has been endorsed by many. Several other labels have been offered, among them Indigenous Americans and Indigenous People. There is no absolute consensus in the matter, even among the first Americans. Currently, Native American is widely used in the media and academia, as well as among some young Indians. It seems also to be favored by certain tribes such as Navajo. Yet one simple fact remains: when Native Americans who live on reservations refer to themselves collectively, most still use, by a large majority, the single word Indians. Indians of any given group, it should be noted, have always and still prefer to be called by their particular tribal name. (Fedullo, 1992)

Throughout this paper, for the reasons stated above, the labels Native Americans, American Indians, and Indians will be used interchangeably.

Furthermore, because a variety of labels are used interchangeably by Native Americans when referring to the mainstream white American population, the terms Anglo, white, dominant culture, mainstream culture, and non-Indian will be used interchangeably.

Acknowledgments

I am pleased to acknowledge the following people for contributing to the completion of this manuscript. Foremost, I wish to recognize my mother who never tired of reading aloud to me and my father who unknowingly instilled Ojibwe ways into the characters of his children. I wish to acknowledge my own children, Bret, Kurt, and Karla, and their schooling experiences that informed my views about how children learn. Appreciation is also due my husband, Jerry, who always encouraged me to take another course, finish another degree. Special recognition is given to my major professor and mathematics educator, Dr. Elizabeth Fennema, for accepting a mathematically phobic educational generalist as an advisee. Likewise, recognition is given to Dr. Robert Clasen for being a friend and guide on the side. I also express appreciation to Genny Gollnick for making it possible for me to complete my study at the Oneida Tribal School. Finally, I wish to acknowledge and thank Ana Alicia for valuing Indian students enough to risk having a researcher in her classroom.

Native American Pedagogy and Cognitive-Based Mathematics Instruction

Chapter 1

Statement of the Problem

Foreshadowing of Culture's Impact

> I never was the greatest mathematician. . . . I never expected to be rich so that I would have to worry about how much money I might get. . . . The father works enough to keep bread on the table, we're fed, we're warm, all of that, but there's no looking down the road to say, "I'm going to have a bicycle by that time." . . . We are never going to be rich because we don't know how to, you know, how to hoard it. When someone needs something and we have it, we'll help. That's the way I am, but I really can't say me, because I'm not me. I am a part of a whole family (Student Advocate 1/1 11-17-73, 275–77, 381–406).
>
> —A 61 year old Oneida teacher

This comment, given in response to the question, "How do you feel about mathematics?" was freely shared by a sixty-one year Oneida school teacher while being interviewed in her home. The home attested to the sincerity of her comment. Though made comfortable with family photos, colorful throws and pillows, and artificial flowers, it spoke boldly against materialism and conspicuous consumption.

I was not surprised with her comment; for most of my life I shared identical feelings. What surprised me was the disregard registered by several mathematics educators after I shared the interview transcription. One comment was, "That's a pretty narrow view of mathematics." I did not disagree with this observation, but I was surprised with the disengagement. More than surprised, I was dismayed that the teacher's comments had not provoked curiosity as to why a sixty-one year old Native American teacher would have held such a narrow mathematics perspective.

My belief is that insight to understanding the mathematical underachievement of many Native American people is sequestered within this teacher's response.

Documentation of the Indian Mathematics Problem

Poor performance and limited participation in mathematics by Native Americans has been well documented throughout the nation (Cajete 1988; Preston 1991; Hadfield 1992). In a paper prepared for a mathematics equity conference, Johnson (1982) reported that while 30.3% of all white students nationally take six or more semesters of math in grades ten through twelve, only 10.9% of all Indians did so. This compares to 17.3 of all Hispanic students and 19.4% of all black students. A comprehensive study completed in 1983 indicated that American Indians were 1.7 years behind the national norm in grade six mathematics achievement and three years behind the norm at grade twelve, and the proportion of Indian students with special needs increased from 32% in grade two to 41% in grade four and 46% in grade six (Fletcher 1983).

Another study with Ute students in northeastern Utah (Leap 1988) helps illuminate how limited mathematics proficiency among primary and secondary Indian students impacts on Indian people in general. Leap concluded that poor mathematics performance extends beyond ineffective problem solving to affective domains as well. He found that Indian children who remain in school (as many as 80% of students on Indian reservations do not complete high school (Fries 1987)) tended to avoid enrolling in mathematics courses or in other courses where mathematics held a significant role in course content. Career choices were also made along similar lines with Ute students rejecting careers that emphasized the need for quantitative skills and favoring career options where qualitative skills were stressed. Consequently, virtually no member of the Northern Ute tribe had been educated in mathematics related sciences, in engineering, in energy-related science, or in business management. It is important to note that this situation is common among tribes across the nation and has serious implications for economic self-determination as well as political self-sufficiency for all American Indians (Lane 1988). Leap concluded his report with the following comment:

> Perhaps it is now clear why the "Indian mathematics problem" continues to be a source of major concern for all Indian educators, and even when the "problem" is recognized; truly effective remediation strategies have yet to emerge (Leap 1982, 185).

As indicated above, a considerable amount of research has documented the Indian mathematics problem and its consequences; however, few studies have focused on the cause and resolution of the problem (Cheek, Scott, and Fletcher 1983). Among the limited studies contributing to this critical discourse are investigations into the influence of low expectations for Indian students held by teachers, counselors, principals (Nash 1973; Green et al. 1978), and parents (Ortiz-Franco 1981); investigations into the impact of equity and opportunity and the influence of low socio-economic status on performance (Witthun 1984); investigations into cognition and learning style aspects (Lombardi 1970; Jordan and Tharp 1979; Rhodes 1989; Tharp 1994) and investigations into social-cultural influences (Guilmet 1979; Philips 1983; Greenbaum 1983; Ericksen and Mohatt , Leap, Spanos 1988).

The present study contributes to this critical discourse by investigating, like Leap, the impact of culture. However, the present study does not implicate culture or call for truly effective remediation strategies as did Leap. Instead, it ethnographically investigates the interactive relationship of one teacher's personal culture-based values and how those values influenced her production of culturally responsive pedagogy. Simply put, the purpose of this investigation was to identify methods of teaching that, because of their cultural congruence, enhance the way Native American children learn mathematics.

Educational researchers, until recently, minimized the importance of investigating the influence of culture on teaching and learning; however, for more than a decade anthropologists have examined ways that teaching can better match the home and community cultures of students of color (Ladson-Billings 1994). Au and Jordon (1981) investigated what came to be termed "culturally appropriate" pedagogy in Hawaiian schools; Cazden and Leggett (1981) and Ericksen and Mohatt (1981) used the term "culturally congruent" to describe interactions of teachers with Native American students; Jordon (1985) and Vogt et al. (1987) used the term "culturally compatible" to explain successful teaching practice of classroom teachers with Native Hawaiian children; later, Erickson and Mohatt (1985) introduced the concept of "culturally responsive" pedagogy. Ladson-Billings (1994), in her article, *Toward a Theory of Culturally Relevant Pedagogy*, stressed that the terms culturally appropriate, culturally congruent, and culturally compatible connote accommodation of student culture to mainstream culture and that only the term "culturally responsive" refers to the dynamic and synergistic relationship between home/community culture and school culture. The present study attempts to advance the investigation of culturally responsive pedagogy.

The Impact of Culture: An Indian Perspective

> When people experience what is called "culture shock" on going from one society to another, it's probably not the obvious differences, which cause the greatest sense of personal disorganization. In other words, it is probably not the differences in physical landscape, climate, religion, dress, or even food, which bring about the strongest sense of confusion. More often, it is in the assumptions of everyday life, shared by members of a society by virtue of constant interaction from birth, assumptions which are so much a part of the culture that they are not even consciously held (Watson 1974, 29).

In every society, children engage in experiences and interactions, which transmit the values, beliefs, and attitudes of that society. Social interactions, which impact directly on math-related attitudes, might be as subtle as whether a child's efforts are rewarded with an appreciative smile or with a monetary allowance. They might be obvious but informal as when a grandfather helps a young gardener estimate distance between rows of beans, or they might be obvious and formal as when a classroom teacher administers a standardized test. It is through such interactions that both spoken and unspoken cultural beliefs and values are communicated and children become enculturated. Understanding this process is intuitively and logically sensible, yet too often the implications of the process are ignored, and too often in mainstream school settings where ethnicities merge, culturally based beliefs and behaviors create misunderstanding and conflict.

Within the past twenty years Indian and non-Indian educators, responding to conflict by recognizing the importance of providing culturally sensitive curriculum, have produced units of study, rewritten textbooks, and infused Indian arts and crafts into lessons. However, large numbers of Indian children continue to underachieve, fail, and drop out of school. Apparently, it is not enough to depict history with an alternative perspective of manifest destiny or to study the geometry involved in basket weaving. It is not that curriculum adaptation is inappropriate. It is simply inadequate. The simple revision of a story or the inclusion of Plains Indian geometric designs will not alter subtle enculturated beliefs. This line of reasoning leads one to wonder whether there are, among American Indians, "assumptions of everyday life" related specifically to mathematics avoidance "which are so much a part of the culture that they are not even consciously held" as Watson suggested? If so, what are they?

One example of a conscious assumption related to mathematics avoidance among Indians was documented by Cocking, Chipman (1992) and Green (1978). These studies report that among Native Americans there is a negative image of mathematics, whereby mathematicians are perceived as remote, competitive, self-serving, obsessive, and calculating. Opposed to this view of mathematicians are fundamental Indian beliefs and values, which are presently shared and have been shared by tribes across the nation for hundreds of years. These values underlie the teacher's comments presented at the beginning of this chapter and include valuing cooperation rather than competition and believing in close family solidarity with mutual support among kinfolk rather than materialism (Butterfield 1985; Phillips 1983; Erickson and Mohatt 1982; Fuchs and Havighurst 1973). Recognition of these fundamental values and acknowledgment of the often competitive and individualistic achievement demands common in dominant American society and reflected often in mainstream mathematics classrooms (Allison and Spence 1993; Romberg 1992), helps one better understand why an Indian student might find it difficult to become excited about planning a mathematics career or even participating in the discourse of a norm-based and competition-driven mathematics classroom. Careful consideration of the mathematics avoidance of Indian people helps illuminate why general instructional efforts of Indian children by non-Indians have failed; the cultural values on which such efforts have been and are based may be in stark contrast to Native American values.

Chapter 2

A Literature Review of Native American Pedagogy and Cognitively Guided Instruction

The Native American Way of Teaching

> Surprisingly little attention has been given to the teaching methods used in teaching ethnic minority students in this country, particularly when the notion of culturally relevant curriculum materials has been around as long as it has. It is as if we have been able to recognize that there are cultural differences in what people learn, but not in how they learn. (Philips 1982)

The preceding quote will serve as a lens through which this chapter is focused. Here, Philips succinctly identifies the critical issue addressed within this study—the importance of culturally compatible teaching methods.

It is this issue that underlies the initial research question: What cultural values influence Oneida instruction? And it is this issue that grounds the investigation of pedagogical compatibility between a Native American way of teaching and Cognitively Guided Instruction (CGI). Within this chapter both Native American pedagogy and

Cognitively Guided Instruction will be described and the commonalties between the two will be identified.

However, before one is able to gain an understanding of traditional Indian teaching, it is important to discuss the Native American perspective of the learner's role. Tafoya (1982) helps illuminate this perspective by relating the incident of a Navajo elder responding to a young boy's query as to why it snows in Montezuma Canyon. The elder responded by telling him a story about a boy who discovered a strange flaming object:

> They (the Holy People) would not allow him to keep even a part of it, but instead put him to a series of tests. When he was successful at these tests, they promised they would throw all of the ashes from their fireplace into Montezuma Canyon each year. "Sometimes they fail to keep their word, and sometimes, they throw down too much; but in all, they turn their attention toward us regularly, here in Montezuma Canyon" (27).

When the boy heard the story, he accepted the explanation of why it snowed in Montezuma Canyon but then wanted to know why it snowed in Blanding, another Navajo area.

> The old man quickly replied, "I don't know. You'll have to make up your own story for that." To the anthropologist (Toelken) who had witnessed this exchange, the old man later commented that, "It was too bad the boy did not understand stories," and he explained that this was not really about the historical origin of snow in Montezuma Canyon or any other place, but a story about the proper reciprocal relationship between man and other beings. He attributed the boy's failure to grasp the meaning of the story to the influence of white schooling (28).

Tafoya's explanation of this interchange situates the learner as an active participant, not merely a passive recipient of knowledge:

> This is very much a part of Native American teaching: that one's knowledge must be obtained by the individual . . . gaining of that knowledge does not come from only listening to elders, or seeing what others have done. . . . The seeker must open up himself to himself . . . . The insights and comprehensions must be achieved internally (28).

Others (Leavitt 1983; Smith 1987; Scollon and Scollon 1981) have investigated both the social and cognitive aspects of storytelling as well as other traditional Native American teaching practices, and, like Tafoya, have concluded that abstracting basic rules and principles is left to participants according to their experience levels and perspectives.

This conclusion situates the learner not as a dependent student but as an autonomous learner. Understanding this perspective becomes vitally important when analyzing principles of Native American pedagogy; learner autonomy is covertly embedded in indirect, cooperative, sense-making, culturally situated, and time-generous instruction.

In the following section, four research studies detailing instruction of Indian children by Indian teachers will be reviewed. Though the studies share attributes common to traditional Native American instruction, such as the autonomous role of the learner, each study was selected to exemplify a particular component or principle of such pedagogy, and each study is identified by the principle it exemplifies:

1. Teacher as facilitator—indirect rather than direct instruction
2. Sense-making instruction
3. Problem-based instruction with problems situated in the culture and lived experiences of the learner
4. Cooperative rather than competitive instruction
5. Time-generous rather than time-driven instruction

Teacher as Facilitator: Indirect Rather Than Direct Instruction

Ericks-Brophy and Crago (1993) analyzed classroom discourse in six Inuit-taught kindergarten and first-grade classrooms in northern Quebec. The findings of this study suggest that unlike mainstream classrooms based on behaviorist learning theory where discourse is typically organized around elicitation sequences initiated and controlled by the teacher (Cazden 1988; Silliman and Wilkinson 1991), Inuit teachers facilitated group responses and peer modeling to decentralize teacher intervention and de-emphasize the authoritarian role of the teacher. The emphasis in the Inuit classrooms was on listening to others as opposed to individual responses and performance. This allowed teachers to capitalize on using peer models to provide correct responses and thus to correct errors. In their interviews, the teachers described their role in terms of the facilitation of peer exchanges:

- to encourage my students to get along and help each other
- that my students learn to cooperate
- that my students respect each other
- to keep all the children equal
- to be a good example to my students

The researchers suggested that this interaction pattern is culturally congruent with the larger Inuit society where individual speakers do not control conversational topics and verbal interactions are typically focused on the general audience and do not tend to spotlight individual participants. They concluded:

> Teachers avoided singling students out for evaluation, praise or correction in front of their peers and were careful not to emphasize or spotlight individual performance in the public arena, allowing students to participate equally in classroom exchanges without pressure or loss of face. In this way, students were able to take greater responsibility for their own learning and the progress of the group. At the same time, they learned central Inuit values concerning the importance of group cooperation, the equality of all group members, and respect for others.

The findings of this study are consistent with those previously outlined in other Native American education studies (Erickson and Mohatt 1982; Foster 1989; Lipka 1991; Philips 1983; Scollon and Scollon 1981). The facilitating teacher role promotes both autonomous and cooperative learning: students take greater responsibility for their own learning as well as the progress of the group.

Problem Solving Based on Sense-making: Each Student Allowed to Solve Problems Any Way That Makes Sense to the Student and Content Situated Within the Lived Experiences of the Learner and Culturally Contextualized

In a case study of a Yup'ik teacher, Lipka (1991) proposes that Yup'ik teachers should teach Yup'ik students. He states that ethnicity is not merely a classroom variable but that it determines the actual interaction style and relationship between students and teachers. He argues that for teachers to effectively instruct, they must possess not only an in-depth understanding of content in the culture, but that they must also share culturally determined communication styles and values. Lipka grounds his proposal on cognitive learning theory:

> Research on minority and indigenous school-aged students reveals a "relational" cognitive style. . . . (This) style recognizes the importance of the whole and the context as opposed to an "analytical" cognitive style, which is abstract and decontextualized (Cohen 1969). . . . The non-Yup'ik teacher states in a linear manner, first this, and then this (Good and Brophy 1987), prior to doing anything. The verbal messages are decontextualized from the content. . . . Differences in ordering of introductory statements between Anglo and Yup'ik teachers are not mere happenstance; they are culturally grounded in Yup'ik and mainstream American culture. Activities (in indigenous classrooms) begin without the customary lengthy verbal introduction Anglos expect. This suggests differences in cognitive ordering and structuring.

Lipka illuminates the intentionality of Native American instruction by explaining specific practices. For example, Native American teachers will ignore requests for procedural or location assistance so as not to reinforce dependence on verbal instruction during lessons that call for observation. Students are also allowed to move from their seats to get a closer look at what other students might be doing. In these ways, the teacher shares the instructional load with the students and builds group solidarity.

Another Native teaching practice is the avoidance of correcting someone or directly telling them that they are wrong. In Yup'ik pedagogy, corrections are based on affirmations of what the student knows. Underlying this practice is the belief that each student is capable of learning when allowed to perform in his/her comfort zone.

In the Yup'ik classroom of this case study, Lipka described instruction as relaxed, almost informal, and reminiscent of lessons taught by elders. The teacher involved the students with content exploration by situating it pedagogically within the lived experiences of the students. Among the examples of situated pedagogy described by Lipka is an incident when the teacher invited the students to sit on the floor with him, some chose to and some chose not to do so. There was no coaxing or statements of persuasion. From a Yup'ik cultural perspective, what was done respected the individual and reinforced group harmony.

Likewise, the lesson content, an art lesson in which the problem to be solved was that of simulating the stretching of a beaver skin, was situated within the Yup'ik culture and required special understanding by the teacher, understanding that perceived the lesson as an art activity as well as a lesson about survival, patience, care, and doing things properly.

To summarize, for instruction to be culturally sensitive, content and pedagogy cannot be separated. Other researchers reporting similar findings include Gilliland (1992), Macias, Ross, and Swisher and Dehyle (1989).

Cooperative Self-determination

Philips (1983) in her book, *The Invisible Culture*, provides a detailed description of how classroom communication patterns of Indian children parallel adult communication patterns on the Warm Springs Indian Reservation in Oregon. Thought provoking findings of this study include:

> Indian students generally make less effort than Anglo students do to get the floor in classroom interaction. They compete with one another less for the teacher's attention, and make less use of the classroom interaction framework to demonstrate academic achievement (108).
>
> It is generally the case that turns at talk are more evenly distributed in Indian classrooms (113).

> In the Indian classroom it is common for children who had demonstrated the ability to answer correctly a particular question in one instance to refrain from even trying to answer the same question the next time it was raised (113).
>
> The children are raised in an environment that discourages drawing attention to oneself by acting as though one is better than another (118).
>
> Indian student verbal participation in-group projects were not only much greater than in whole class or small-group (teacher directed) encounters, but also qualitatively different. As a rule, one could not determine who had been appointed as leaders of the Indian groups on the basis of the organization of interaction, and when the students were asked to pick a leader, they usually ignored the instructions and got on to the task at hand (120).
>
> Indian children demonstrate a strong preference for team games and races . . . but they show a reluctance to function as leaders in games that require one person to control the activities of others (122).
>
> In group projects and playground activities, Indian students were able to sustain infrastructure interactions involving more students for a longer time (compared to white students in the same study) without the interaction breaking down because of conflict or too many people trying to control the talk (124).

In her study, Philips proposes that the non-competitive, cooperative nature of Indian children is behavior, which mirrors adult communication patterns. She hypothesizes that Indian organization of interaction can be characterized as maximizing the control that an individual has over his or her own talk, and as minimizing the control that a given individual has over others. Furthermore, she explains that Indians are not accustomed to having to appeal to a single individual for permission to speak but rather determining for themselves whether they will speak. Indians would consider behavior, which might be judged by Anglos to be reticent and insecure, as self-determining.

Many studies of North American Indians have noted that overt authority, which would interfere with the autonomy of the individual, is rarely or never exercised (Basso 1970; Erickson and Mohatt 1982; Hallowell 1955; Spindler and Spindler 1971).

It is not that Indians are by nature self-effacing, rather, Philips suggests that this behavior is consequential to the caretaking patterns of extended families. A child cared for by siblings and cousins is less likely to compete for the attention of a dominant adult and is more likely to attend to the rhythms of group interaction while maintaining a healthy degree of independence. "The notion of a single individual being structurally set apart from all others, in anything other than an observer role, and yet still a part of the group organization, is one that Indian children probably encounter for the first time in school (Philips 1972)."

Time-generous Rather than Time-driven

Erickson and Mohatt (1982) investigated the interaction patterns of two-experienced first grade teachers, one Indian and one Anglo, in Odawa and Ojibwe classrooms in Northern Ontario. A significant contribution of this study was the comparison of time allocation for instructional activities between the classrooms. The study documented that the Indian teacher spent more time waiting for students to finish their work—students were given 15 minutes to finish work in the Indian classroom and an average of 5 minutes in the Anglo classroom, that the Indian teacher appeared to accommodate more sensitively to the children's rates of beginning, doing and finishing work, and that she maintained control of the students not with overt directives but by paying close attention to the rhythms of activity and judging when the students were ready for things to change.

The researchers explained this behavior as reflecting sensitivity to culturally valued collaborative behavior, rather than to authoritarianism. The Indian teacher's strategies involved proceeding fairly slowly and deliberately, sharing the social control—leadership shared by teacher and by students rather than divided into separate compartments: teacher time and student time. The teacher had control of the students but achieved this by paying close attention to each student's progress. In this way, the students clearly had control of the teacher. A predetermined schedule or curriculum agenda directed by the teacher did not set the pace for instruction.

Lipka (1991) reported similar findings in the study described above. He explained that Indian students have a different set of "rights and responsibilities" than we would find in a mainstream classroom.

They begin and finish a task at their own pace, within the confines of school. The teacher does not say, "Okay, it's three o'clock and it's time to leave, everybody hand in your work." The task and the involvement of the children with the task determined time. Gilliland (1992), in his book *Teaching the Native American*, explains:

> The Native American characteristic which is probably most misunderstood is their concept of time. To European-Americans, time is very important. It must be used to the fullest. Hurry is the by-word. Get things done. They feel guilty if they are idle. They say, "Time flies." To the Mexican, "time walks." However, the Indian tells me, "Time is with us." Life should be easy going, with little pressure. There is no need to watch clocks. In fact, many Indian languages have no word for time. Things should be done when they need to be done. Exactness of time is of little importance. When an activity should be done is better determined by when the thing that precedes it is completed or when circumstances are right than by what the clock says (32–33).

Summary

> Culture is a system of standards for perceiving, believing, evaluating, and acting (Goodenough 1971).

> People in interaction are environments for each other. (McDermott 1976).

Integration of these two quotes undergirds the underlying premise presented at the beginning of this study and elaborated within this section: culturally sensitive classroom environments are those in which ways of perceiving, believing, acting, and evaluating are shared. For Native American children, such classrooms are grounded on the following pedagogical principles:

1. Teacher as facilitator—indirect rather than direct instruction
2. Problem solving based on sense making—each student is allowed to solve problems any way that makes sense to that student
3. Problem-based instruction with problems situated in the culture and lived experiences of the learner

4. Cooperative rather than competitive instruction
5. Time-generous rather than time-driven instruction

Cognitively Guided Instruction: A Culturally Sensitive Mathematics Approach for Primary Age Native American Children

Cognitively Guided Instruction (CGI) developed out of a mathematics research project at the University of Wisconsin-Madison. This approach has been shown to be highly successful for developing number sense with mainstream as well as minority children (Carey, Fennema, Carpenter, and Franke 1993; Villasenor 1992), and is recognized as a program that complies with national mathematics reform standards (NCTM 1989).

A major attribute that sets CGI apart from other mathematics approaches is that it does not prescribe instruction or provide instructional materials. Rather, it helps teachers learn about the relation between the structure of primary level mathematics and children's thinking of that mathematics. The goal of this approach is that teachers will be able to understand how their children learn mathematics concepts and that this knowledge will inform instruction (Carpenter and Fennema 1992).

Content shared during extended CGI workshops is built on research which identified regularities in children's solutions to different types of mathematical story problem situations when children were allowed to solve problems intuitively rather than following a teacher imposed procedure, (Carpenter 1985; Fuson 1992; Streeflan 1993). Of importance to the present study is the fact that children from other culture groups: Hispanic children (Villasenor 1992), African American children (Carey 1993), and Lebanese children (Ghaleb 1992), demonstrated the same regularities in their solutions; apparently, learners across cultures share similar cognitive processes when intuitively solving mathematical story problems.

CGI research is also based on a detailed analysis of content domains: basic addition, subtraction, multiplication, and division problem situations are separated into several basic classes, which are distinguished by different mathematical relationships. This scheme provides a framework for systematically generating a complete taxonomy of mathematical word problems that distinguishes among problems in terms of difficulty (*see* Problem Types, Appendix A).

Additionally, the taxonomy of problem types provides a framework to identify the developmental cognitive processes that children use to solve problems: when children begin to solve problems, they concretely represent the relationships in the problem; over time, concrete strategies are abstracted to counting strategies and the use of derived facts (*see* Solution Strategies, Appendix A). Summarily, this research-based perspective provides the teacher with a coherent analysis of the structure of the mathematics as well as the developmental strategies that children use when acquiring the ability to solve mathematical problems.

Over time, Cognitively Guided Instruction promotes a cumulative process of mathematical understanding for the learner: place value concepts and multidigit operations become natural extensions of the processes children use to solve more basic problems; operations and multidigit numbers follow a similar pattern of understanding based on experiences with smaller numbers; and children's development of initial fraction concepts emerge through their partitioning strategies applied when solving partitive division problems (Carpenter et al. 1993).

Over time, Cognitively Guided Instruction also promotes a cumulative process of mathematical understanding for the teacher. A willingness on the part of the teacher to listen to the voices of her/his students when attempting to understand their thinking promotes the teacher's understanding of mathematics. Stated another way, the experience of applying the research-based knowledge introduced in a CGI workshop, posing taxonomically structured problems to students and attending to their solutions, enables the teacher to explore other mathematical content (telling time, geometry, measurement) through the eyes of the student.

What CGI Looks Like in the Classroom

Even though CGI does not prescribe instruction, CGI classrooms do have similarities. Children in these classrooms spend most of their time solving problems. Usually, problems are related to a book the teacher has read to the class, a theme or unit being studied outside of mathematics class, or something going on in the lives of the students. Various physical materials are available to children to assist them in solving problems. Each child decides how to solve a problem, which may include using materials, such as manipulatives and/or paper and pencils, or solving a problem mentally. Children are not shown how to solve problems. Instead, each child solves them any way that s/he can, often in more than one way, and shares how the problem was solved with peers and the teacher. The group listens and questions until they understand the strategy the child used. Then other children share their solution strategies. The entire process is repeated with another problem. Using information of each child's reporting of a problem solution, teachers make decisions about what each child knows and how instruction should be structured to enable that child to learn.

The climate of a CGI classroom is one in which each person's thinking is important and respected by the group. Children approach problem solving willingly and recognize that their thinking is critical. Each child is perceived to be in charge of his or her own learning, as individual knowledge of mathematics is used to solve problems that are realistic and relevant (Carey, Fennema, Carpenter, and Franke 1993). The following excerpt, from an article written by the developers of Cognitively Guided Instruction (Carpenter and Fennema 1992), reports the findings of a CGI teacher study and details instructional principles of this approach.

> The critical element in the classes in which we observed the most impressive levels of problem solving was that the teachers were able to assess what their students were capable of so that they could continue to expand the students' knowledge by giving them increasingly challenging problems that were not beyond their capabilities. By listening to their students, these teachers learned that their students were capable of solving much more challenging problems than they previously anticipated. They did not simply give increasingly more difficult problems; they were able to match the problems to the students' abilities. To assess their students, the teachers did not rely on written tests or formal assessment procedures. Instead assessment was an ongoing part of instruction. The teachers continually asked their students to describe the processes they had used to solve a given problem. The teachers almost never taught a lesson designed to teach specific procedures. In-group discussions they almost always asked students to explain how they solved a particular problem, and students always were encouraged to describe alternative solutions. Typically four or five different students would describe how they had solved a problem. In individual or small group work, the teacher also asked students to explain their work rather than showing them what they did wrong. The

following protocol of a teacher working with a group of five (first grade) students illustrates how a CGI teacher gives children an opportunity to discuss alternative solutions.

> *Ms. M.:* "The African Elephant ate 37 peanuts. The Indian Elephant ate 43 peanuts. How many fewer peanuts did the African elephant eat than the Indian Elephant?"

The children worked on the problem for two and a half minutes. Some of the children used stacking cubes that had been joined together in stacks of ten cubes. Others did not use any materials. After a minute and a half several of the children had raised their hands. After two minutes, only one child, Ubank, was still working on the problem. Ms. M. asked him if he was done. When he shook his head, she told him to keep working. After another half minute he raised his hand.

> *Ms. M.:* "Got it? How many fewer did the African Elephant eat, Ubank?"
>
> *Ubank:* "Six."
>
> *Ms. M.:* "Does everyone agree with that? . . . How did you figure it out, Ubank?"
>
> *Ubank:* "Well, I had 43 here (pushing out 4 stacks of ten cubes and 3 additional cubes joined together), and I had 37 here (pushing out 3 stacks of ten cubes and a stack of 7). I put 30 on top of these 30. I took 3 and I put them here. There were 4 left, so I took off 4, and there were 6 left."

As he described what he did, he took 3 of the ten stacks from the collection of 43 and put them on top of the 3 ten stacks in the collection of 37. Then he took the three single cubes from the original set of 43 and put them on top of the 7 cubes in the set of 37. Then he took the remaining stack of ten cubes from the original 43 and broke off 4 cubes. He put these 4 cubes on the 4 cubes in the set of 37 that were not covered. He was left with 6 cubes from the set of 43 that did not match up with cubes in the set of 37.

> *Ms. M.:* "Did he do it a good way? . . . Did anyone do it a different way?
>
> *Marci:* "I took 37, and I needed 43. So I counted up 3 more. That was 40. Then I took 3 more to 43."
>
> *Ms. M.:* "Good. Does her way work well? . . . It sure does. Did anyone do it differently?"
>
> *Linda:* "Well, first I got 37. Then I got 43 (pushes out collections of 37 and 43 cubes joined together in stacks of ten with the extra cubes also joined together). See, I know it couldn't be 10. So what I did was I imagined 3 more cubes here (points to the top of the stack of 7 cubes in the set of 37), and I imagined 3 more right here (pointing to a space next to the collection of 37 that corresponds to where the 3 cubes are in the collection of 43).

Ms. M. gave each child in the group time to complete the problem, and she gave each child who had a different solution an opportunity to explain his or her solution. The children all listened attentively to other children's solutions, so the children had the chance to learn from each other. Ms. M. also learned what each child could do, and she learned more than whether the child got the correct answer.

Careful reflection on the principles of Native American pedagogy outlined in the previous section and the preceding description of a CGI classroom leads one to recognize commonalties between the two approaches, such commonalties are compared in Table 1.

Table 1: Correspondence between Native American Pedagogy and Cognitively Guided Instruction

Native American Culture-based Instruction Principle #1	**CGI Example**
Teacher as facilitator - indirect rather than direct instruction	The teacher presents problems and trusts students to solve them. Students are encouraged to construct their own under-standing as well as instruct one another.

Table 1 (cont.)

Native American Culture-based Instruction Principle #2	**CGI Example**
Problem solving that is sense making (each student is allowed to solve problems in any way that makes sense to that student)	Students are allowed to use tools in any way that makes sense to them, i. e., manipulating concrete objects, drawing, invented procedures, etc.
Native American Culture-based Instruction Principle #3	**CGI Example**
Problems based culturally and on the lived experiences of the students.	Problems are based on shared classroom experience, e.g. a story, a science unit, students' lives.

Native American Culture-based Instruction Principle #4	**CGI Example**
Cooperation rather than competition	Children are allowed to work in teams or individually and are asked to share their solution strategies. Each student's thinking is accepted and respected.
Native American culture-based Instruction Principle #5	**CGI Example**
Time generous rather than time driven instruction	Class time is spent solving several complex problems with understanding. Enough time is granted to discuss problems thoroughly.

Native American Storytelling and CGI

At this point it is important to pause and consider: If the Native American way of teaching and CGI share major pedagogical principles, is there anything different between these two approaches, and if so, what is it? To answer this, I refer to the traditional Native American art of storytelling. Gollnick (1993) explained that the power of storytelling resides in the teller's ability to adjust the story to the listener's level of understanding. She explained further that a story can be told at many levels, from very simple to philosophically abstract. She concluded that a good storyteller knows both the story and the listener. Herein lies the key to distinguishing Cognitively Guided Instruction from Native American pedagogy. A CGI teacher knows the "story" of mathematics as well as the developmental levels of understanding that children pass through when learning mathematics; the CGI teacher, like a good storyteller, is able to adjust the problems posed according to the levels of the children's understanding. However, specific mathematics content knowledge is not part of Native American pedagogy. Consequently, a teacher who values the principles of Native American pedagogy but is mathematically insecure, may rely on a culturally insensitive mathematics textbook when making instructional decisions.

Furthermore, though the principles of instruction of these two approaches are similar, their derivations and uses are very different. Native American pedagogy derives from the cultural values of Indian people and is applied in a general way to instruction across content. The principles of Cognitively Guided Instruction derive from the integration of two bodies of knowledge: the knowledge of the structure of primary level mathematics and the ways that children think about that mathematics. It is the integration of these two bodies of knowledge that transforms mathematics instruction and produces a pedagogy that is time-generous, cooperative, and learner situated.

Theoretically, primary level Indian educators who value and practice Native American pedagogy will be culturally advantaged when learning and using CGI; they already value the instructional principles, but what most do not possess is the structural knowledge of mathematics and knowledge of children's thinking about mathematics. Cognitively Guided Instruction provides opportunities to acquire that knowledge.

The Cultural Relevance of CGI Content

An important question that must be addressed is whether the mathematics valued by CGI developers is culturally relevant for Indian people. I choose to postpone discussing this query until providing additional information about a scholarly shift in the philosophy of mathematics epistemology and pedagogy, a shift which impacted directly on the development of Cognitively Guided Instruction.

Significant changes have occurred regarding beliefs held by mathematics educators in national institutions about the nature of mathematics, the way it is used, and the way it is learned. Mathematics is no longer thought to be a fixed body of knowledge organized hierarchically. Instead, it is viewed as a changing product of human invention (Ernest 1991), as a process of inquiry that involves human creativity, and as a system for solving real problems (National Research Council [NCR] 1990). Likewise, many believe that mathematics instruction should shift from being teacher directed to being learner directed: learning is no longer considered a process of passively absorbing information and storing it in easily retrievable fragments as a result of repeated practice and reinforcement. Instead, it is now recognized that students approach each new task with some prior knowledge, assimilate new information, and construct their own meanings (Resnick 1987; Romberg and Carpenter 1986). These philosophical and learning theory changes influence the current national mathematics reform movement advanced by the National Council of Teachers of Mathematics and described in the *Curriculum and Evaluation Standard for School Mathematics* (1989) and NCTM *Professional Standards for Teaching Mathematics* (1991). However, a much broader shift underlies this change of mathematics philosophy and this shift is grounded on the projected societal needs of the twenty-first century:

> Schools, as now organized, are a product of the industrial age. In most democratic countries, common schools were created to provide most youth the training needed to become workers in fields, factories, and shops. As a result of such schooling, students also were expected to become literate enough to be informed voters. Thus, minimum competencies in reading and writing, and arithmetic were expected of all students, and more advanced academic training was reserved for the select few. These more advanced students attended the schools that were expected to educate the future cultural, academic, business, and government leaders.
>
> The educational system of the industrial age does not meet the economic needs of today. New social goals for education include :
>
> 1. Mathematically literate workers,

2. Lifelong learning,
3. Opportunity for all, and
4. An informed electorate.

> Implicit in these goals is a school system organized to serve as an important resource for all citizens throughout their lives (NCTM *Standards* 1989, 3).

Having reflected on the shift in learning theory as well as the shift in national schooling expectations and how both relate to mathematics instruction, it is time to return to the question that started this discussion, Is Cognitively Guided Instruction relevant for Indian children? To answer this, one must rely on input from members of Indian communities to decide first whether and what mathematics is valued.

Foster (1989) interviewed Ojibwe elders at the Bad River Reservation in Wisconsin to determine what mathematics they felt were important for Indian children to learn in school. The elders clearly perceived a need for children to learn mathematics both for their individual economic well being and for tribal survival in a bicultural setting. Lane (1988) emphasized the importance of mathematics competence among Indian people for economic self-determination as well as political self-sufficiency. Apparently, Native American mathematics is the same as the dominant culture mathematics in the sense that both culture groups exist in a technologically advanced world in which all people are confronted daily with complex math problems. Avoiding math in the twenty-first century is practically impossible.

The problem-based, sense-making mathematics of Cognitively Guided Instruction is a mathematics that has been identified by mathematics educators as relevant for twenty-first century learners, and since today's Native American children are twenty-first century learners, it can be generalized that CGI content is relevant for them. So, the question changes from whether Cognitively Guided Instruction mathematics is relevant for Indian children, to whether this cognitive approach to teaching mathematics is culturally appropriate for Indian children.

Chapter 3

Design of the Study

This chapter reports the qualitative methodology employed in the study. The report includes: details of the thematic analysis of culture-focused interviews used to identify Oneida values, descriptions of the process of documenting classroom instruction and determining the correspondence between Native American pedagogy and Cognitively Guided Instruction, and an overview of the process of administering and analyzing clinical student interviews used to document the influence of Cognitively Guided Instruction on Oneida kindergartners' mathematical problem-solving ability. The chapter begins with a discussion of personal intuitions that drove the investigation and a description of the obstacles that threatened, early on, to terminate the study.

Pursuing the Investigation

After working with the Cognitively Guided Instruction project for four months as a project assistant, I became intuitively convinced that the instructional principles of CGI corresponded with the Native American way of teaching. I trace this conviction to the fact that my father is Ojibwe. Though I did not grow up on a reservation and was educated in mainstream schools, the Indian value system has always influenced me. My unfounded conviction of corresponding pedagogies prompted me to begin my literature review of Native American teaching practices. I also decided that theory validation would require involving Native American teachers of Native American children in the discussion. At first, I thought the investigation would simply be a matter of finding several teachers willing to complete a CGI workshop, implement what they had learned in their instruction, and then rely on their experiences, observations, and comments to confirm or disconfirm my theory.

Within a six-month period, I came to realize the complexity of the study. Two unanticipated obstacles confronted me:

1. Finding Native American teachers willing to participate in a research study; and
2. finding a teacher who was knowledgeable about Native American ways of teaching.

Obstacle One: Locating a Study Site—Building Trust

In the autumn of 1991, driven with almost a missionary zeal, I began plans to involve six Native American teachers in a CGI workshop sponsored by Cray Academy, an industry supported teacher inservice conference, scheduled for the summer of 1992. However, this task proved to be difficult. Tribal School Administrators questioned my intentions. I came to realize that research completed by an outsider was unwanted and that university researchers were viewed with suspicion. For seven months my recruiting attempts were unsuccessful, and I began to fear that I would never find teachers willing to participate.

In desperation, I contacted the American Indian Science and Engineering Society in Boulder, Colorado, to ask whether they had a Wisconsin representative who might help me recruit Indian teachers. I was advised to contact Genny Gollnick, the curriculum coordinator of the Oneida Tribal School near Green Bay, Wisconsin. I phoned to schedule a meeting and briefly explained my purpose and time constraints. As soon as I finished speaking, I was assured that the Oneida school would have at least three teachers who would be willing to participate. I hung up the phone with a sigh of relief. Later, Genny explained that she had been introduced to cognitive learning theory while finishing her masters degree at Harvard during the mid 1980s. At that time she recognized the correspondence between traditional Native American teaching and cognitive theory, and when I explained CGI and what it was that I was attempting to investigate, she immediately understood.

Gaining School Board Consent

The CGI workshop did what I had anticipated, it convinced the three teachers (one kindergarten, one first grade, and one second grade) that there was merit in the approach for teaching mathematics to Native American children. When I spoke with them about being involved in a study documenting the effectiveness of CGI, they were hesitant but agreeable. I promised to make it as painless as possible. At this point, I felt that my major obstacle had been surmounted: I finally had my participating teachers. But, I was wrong. There was yet another hurtle, the study could not be completed without the consent of the school board.

In October, 1992, after observing in the participating teachers' classrooms and receiving teacher affirmation as to the effectiveness of CGI, I arranged to present the study proposal to the school board for approval. I was granted five minutes to speak, and my comments were met with polite silence. I had been advised to excuse myself after the presentation and not to expect an immediate response. Several months passed, and I heard nothing. In spite of this, I visited the participating teachers' classrooms regularly, and during these visits, other teachers and their aids, most of whom had initially seemed remote, began to nod and occasionally smile. I started to feel accepted.

However, smiles and nods do not translate into signed signatures on research human studies consent forms. In March, 1993, my major professor gave me an ultimatum: either get the official consent to complete a dissertation study or find another study. At this point in my graduate program, I had passed my preliminary exam and was in the last semester of coursework. "You know, Judy, you can always continue your work with Native American children after you've finished your Ph.D. What you need is your union card," my major professor counseled. I assured her that during my next visit I would get documented approval.

By this time I had become well acquainted with the curriculum coordinator and regarded her not only as a highly competent educator and Oneida culture expert but also as a friend. I confided my dilemma and asked if there was any way that I could get the school board approval. Genny looked at me and said, "These things take time. The very fact that you are allowed to do what you are doing, visit the classrooms and talk with the teachers, is an indication that you have approval. If it wasn't okay, you would have been shown the door a long time ago." I left her office with mixed feelings. I knew that I was caught between two cultures: one driven by formal policy and another by feelings. Would the feeling culture ever comply with the formal requirements? If not, I would have to find another study. The possibility brought a choking sob to my throat, and when I pushed open the school door into a blustery March afternoon, I started to cry. For me, there was a bigger purpose to this study than merely completing a Ph.D. I couldn't just walk away. Then something happened. After wiping the tears from my eyes, I looked up and into a bare-limbed maple tree; there sat four large black crows. They were not sitting on alternating branches but in a straight line, as though on a pole. This struck me as odd, and I stared at them wondering how a maple branch could hold such large birds in a straight row. Suddenly, my mind was filled with a comforting thought, "I had approval, and I would receive formal approval. I would complete my study, and the findings of this study would benefit Native American children in the four directions of the nation." As this thought filled my mind, the crows lifted from the branch, each flying in a different direction. I was suddenly filled with a sense of sacred assurance. As I stood reflecting on what had happened, I realized that I was standing in the school parking lot and there was no maple tree. The following week, I told my major advisor that I had received formal approval.

Many months later, on October 7, 1993, the curriculum coordinator spoke on my behalf to the Oneida Tribal School Board of Education and requested permission for me to complete my study. During her presentation, she emphasized that, "Judy Hankes has freely given of her time." Permission was granted (Appendix B).

Description of the Study Site

At the time of the study, the K–8 Oneida Tribal School (OTS) was located on the Oneida Reservation in the Norbert Hill Community Center, a large building situated on a hill overlooking woodlands. This building wasn't always a site where Oneida families chose to send their children. During the first half of the century, the center was a Bureau of Indian Affairs boarding school, a place where Indian children were isolated from their families and disciplined for speaking the Oneida language. Two elder Oneida language instructors, a brother and sister who were students at the school during the early boarding school years, shared stories of those years:

> If you spoke Oneida, you were punished. . . . I remember sitting in the sewing room. . . . only three, four, five years old. I had to knit. (That sister) cut a heel out of a sock, and she made me mend that sock. Plus, I've been hit with a ruler like this, you know (slapping the back of her hand). She would hit

> (demonstrating again). . . . I met that lady later, and I said, "I never did like you, Sister." "Why?" she says. "Because you did this and you did that." She says, "I don't recall." I say, "I do." In my little mind, it was a hardship for me, really hard (Elder woman 1/1 11-2-93, 73–96).
>
> —An 82 year old Oneida elder

> The first time I ran away [from the BIA school], the disciplinarian, he went after me on a motorcycle. We only lived about a mile and a half down the line. Later I found out that he used to get a dollar a head bounty. . . . The third time I ran away my grandpa said, "If you can't keep him there, then there must be something wrong someplace." And there was. They wouldn't let you talk, you know, your own language. . . . There was always somebody watching to see if you spoke Oneida, and if they caught you talking Oneida they made you stand on a stool, and them stools had no back on them or nothing, just a plain stool. They would make you stand on a stool and watch the others eat. And you only had so much time that you could be in the dining area, twenty minutes at most, and when they got through eating, you marched out too with your plate still there, but you can't touch it. You walk out of there with an empty stomach (Elder man 1/ 2 11-17-93, 355–64, 375–83).
>
> —An 86 year old Oneida elder

Today, Oneida high school students attend classes in the Norbert Hill Center and K–8 students attend classes in a new and unique school built in the shape of a giant turtle. In both sites the Oneida language is taught; no longer are students hit with rulers or deprived of food for speaking their language, and the school's K–12 mission statement stresses the importance of retaining cultural identity through culturally appropriate education for the purpose of preserving the Oneida community.

Demographic Details

The Oneida Tribe is a member of the Iroquois Confederacy of five nations, which formed in the 1500s. The Iroquois League initially was composed of the Mohawk, Oneida, Onondaga, Cayuga, and Seneca Nations. In the early 1700s the Tuscarora National became a member of what is now known as the Six Nation Confederacy.

The original Iroquois homelands were located in central New York state. However, these lands were gradually lost through various U.S. government land deals, and tribes were forced to relocate. In the 1820s, the Oneida Nation settled about ten miles from the present site of Green Bay, and in 1838 the U.S. government formally signed a treaty recognizing the present boundaries of the Oneida Reservation in Outagamie County and the township of Hobart in Brown County.

In 1934 the Oneidas formed a constitutional government under the Indian Reorganization Act and elected a General Tribal Council. In 1975, after years of tribal government struggle, the Oneidas started to offer services mainly for tribal members through state and federal funded programs. In the 1960s the tribe employed four persons. It now employs more than 600. Employment is in tribal enterprises (approximately 90% of the tribal budget) or by programs funded by State and Federal funds (approximately 10% of the tribal budget). Programs include a comprehensive health center (optical, dental, and out-patient clinic, social services, K–12 tribal school, Headstart and daycare, higher education and career planning, housing, public transit, a museum, and a library. Enterprises include Bingo & Casino, Big Green Lottery, TV Bingo Oneida, a cannery, tobacco outlets, a nursing home, a gift shop, a printing company, four convenience stores, and a 202 room hotel – the Radisson Inn Green Bay.

Obstacle Two: The Native American Way of Teaching—A Lost Pedagogy

A major assumption of this investigation was that there exists shared beliefs among Native Americans about an Indian way of teaching, a way of teaching that could be reflected on when considering the cultural compatibility of Cognitively Guided Instruction.

Early on, I decided to limit my investigation to the study of one teacher and one classroom. After several informal conversations with the carefully selected participant, a kindergarten teacher named Ana, I came to realize that the preceding assumption was invalid. Though Ana appeared to practice instructional routines that corresponded with a Native American way of teaching, she was unable to articulate what she thought a Native American way of teaching might be. When discussing this dilemma with the curriculum coordinator, Genny explained, "Indian teachers and their parents were educated in mainstream schools. Their grandparents were educated in boarding schools where they were taught that the Indian way was wrong. Most tribal teachers have not been expected to consider teaching in any way other than the way they were taught. No one has asked them to think about a culturally compatible way of teaching. If they seem to teach in such a way, it's because it's in them, but most have not consciously thought about it."

During this conversation, I recognized the common experience that had driven me to begin my literature review: I had a sense that there was an Indian way of teaching but did not know what it was. Likewise, though the classroom teacher had been enculturated to hold Indian values, her primary, secondary, and post-secondary schooling had been dictated by the dominant culture. Consequently, she was unable to consider what an Oneida way of teaching might be. I had one major advantage, as a researcher, I was granted the time to reflect on what an Indian way of teaching might be.

Confronted with this unexpected reality, I was forced to drastically change my research methodology from simply assuming the ability of the participating teacher to compare Cognitively Guided Instruction with Oneida and Native American pedagogy to validating the teacher's ability to recognize and discuss what a culturally compatible pedagogy might look like. The study changed in two significant ways: first, before asking the teacher to discuss pedagogic commonalties and cultural correspondence, her level of awareness of Oneida culture beliefs and correspondence of such beliefs with the generic Native American pedagogy described in Chapter Two had to be confirmed. Additionally, the teacher's recognition and articulation of how cultural beliefs influenced her instruction had to be documented. Reflecting on what an Indian way of teaching might be became consequential to the teacher's ability to reflect on and integrate her own cultural beliefs and understandings.

Figure 1

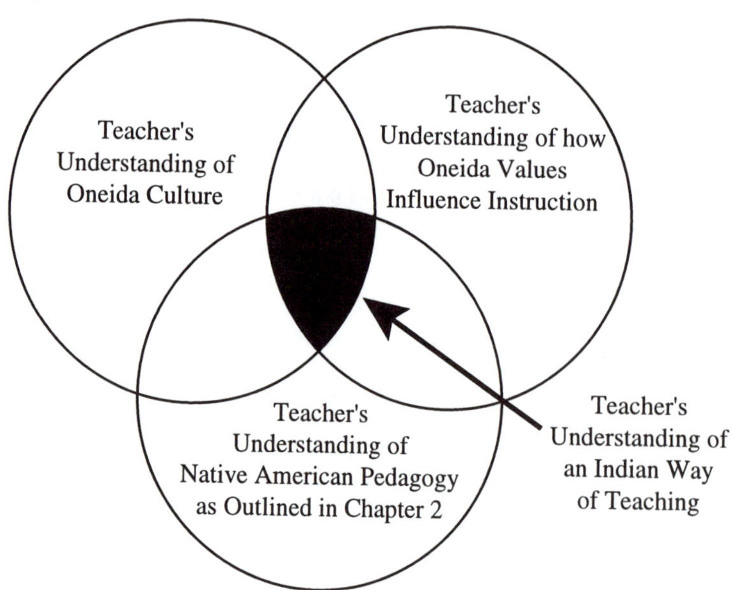

Facilitating the teacher's reflection in this multistep process became part of the organizational structure for this study. First, values unique to Oneida culture had to be identified by the participating teacher and affirmed by other Oneida community members. Next, the teacher had to reflect on and discuss how her culture values influenced her instruction. Additionally, the teacher had to read and reflect on worldview Indian values and how they might inform a generalized Native American pedagogy. These three steps (figure 1) preceded her ability to talk about an Indian way of teaching and to eventually consider whether Cognitively Guided Instruction was compatible with that way.

Identifying Oneida Culture Values

Beliefs and values unique to Oneida culture were identified through interviews with five Oneida community members, four women and one man. A process known as informed subject selection (Spradely 1979) was used to identify participants. In this process, tribal members identified individuals possessing knowledge of the Oneida culture. All participants were members of the Oneida Tribal School education community: two Oneida language instructors, a curriculum coordinator, an advocate for Oneida students enrolled in public schools, and the participating kindergarten teacher.

Culture Interview Procedure

All culture interviews were semistructured. A structured interview had initially been developed; however, direct questions produced short and guarded responses. As an alternative to asking direct questions, each informant was asked to read and react to the Native American Value Scale: a scale based on cross-tribal values (located at the end of this section), the Iroquois Creed: a document displayed in the Tribal School hallway and identified by the school's curriculum coordinator as representative of Oneida values (Appendix C), the Oneida Tribal School Mission Statement (Appendix C), and a list of the Native American pedagogies discussed in Chapter Two. Consequently, interview questions varied from informant to informant.

All interviews took place in private surroundings (a classroom, private office, home, a vacant corner of a restaurant), and all started informally with a brief explanation of the study and the informant being asked to talk about herself/himself. Each interview lasted approximately one hour, and three informants were interviewed on two separate occasions. Two of the five interviews completed with the kindergarten teacher focused on culture. Examples of questions posed during interviews follow (see Appendix D for an interview transcription).

- [Referring to the values scale] Are you saying that cooperation rather than competition is Oneida? [Questions like these were posed after the participant had read and located himself/herself on the scale. The data acquired through this process was not coded or reported. This instrument was used to initiate discussion about Indian values only.]
- You indicated that Oneidas share more than acquire. Is that typical of most Oneida?
- [Referring to the Iroquois Creed] Do you think the Creed reflects the values of the Oneida people?
- Would you tell me about the values and beliefs of Oneida people as you understand them?

- Another part here [reading from the Creed], "He coveted no titles but believed that all men are equal." What do you think about that?
- What do you think was the old way of teaching? How do you think the elders might have taught?
- In many classrooms the teacher stands in the front of the room and tells the children what to do. What do you think about that way of teaching?

Sequence Summary for Developing the Culture Interview

The sequence of events outlining the culture value identification process are summarized in the following six steps:

1. During an informal conversation, I asked the participating teacher what she thought a Native American way of teaching might be. She was unable to respond.
2. A structured interview was developed. During this interview, I asked the teacher to describe what she believed to be Oneida culture values. The teacher's responses were short and guarded.
3. With the help of the Oneida Tribal School curriculum coordinator, I selected three culture documents: the Native American Value Scale, the Oneida Creed, and the Oneida Tribal School Mission Statement.
4. An unstructured interview was developed and completed with the participating teacher. At the beginning of this interview, I asked the teacher to locate herself on the Native American value scale (following page). After completing the scale, we discussed each item and it's correspondence with Oneida culture values.
5. During a second unstructured interview, the teacher was asked to discuss how her culture values influenced her instruction. She was also asked to discuss the correspondence between the Native American pedagogy reported in Chapter 2 and traditional Oneida teaching.
6. Four Oneida elders, educators in the Oneida Tribal school system, were then interviewed. The three culture documents were used in the manner described above to stimulate discussion.

Figure 2: Native American Value Scale

Locate Yourself

	Very Much	A Little	A Little	Very Much	
Acquiring					Sharing
Cooperative					Competitive
Assertive					Passive
Clock-free					Time-driven
Meditative					Impulsive
Joking humor					Subtle humor
Nuclear family					Extended family
Seek control					Seek harmony
Leisure-oriented					Work-oriented
Rational					Intuitive
Spiritual					Logical
Contemporary					Traditional
Round about					Blunt
Individual					Group
achievement					achievement
Slow to warm up					Instant "on"
Personal space needed					Closeness desired
Unstructured					Structured
Parts to whole					Whole to parts

Source: Gilliland, H. *Teaching the Native American.* Dubuque: Kendal Hunt, 1992.

Culture Interview Transcription and Analysis

All interviews were audiotaped and transcribed, generating 150 pages for analysis. I completed all transcriptions. This familiarized me with a general sense of how informants talked about cultural values and which transcribed conversations were culture-value focused. The transcripts were analyzed by reading and rereading to establish close familiarity with the data. This process was completed by hand. First, each transcript was read without attempting to identify culture themes. Next, each was reread and comments related to Oneida beliefs and values (i.e., family, Creator, sharing) were circled and labeled. Labeled transcripts were then cut apart and sorted: all comments related to sharing were placed in one pile; all comments related to the family were placed in another pile, etc. In this way, emergent cultural themes were categorized and identified. These themes were modified and reclassified as a result of active searches for disconfirming and confirming evidence found in the data (i.e., since all informants identified spirituality as a value shared by Oneida people, transcripts were reread to determine whether this value was mentioned but regarded as insignificant in modern Oneida culture). This process led to theme refinements and the development of four culture value categories: the importance of spirituality, the importance of harmony, the importance of generosity, and the importance of cooperation (Appendix E). As an example, the following comment was selected from the curriculum coordinator's transcribed interview as confirming evidence for the existence of spirituality and the belief in the Creator Spirit:

> They [Indians] look at a white person coming in as another human being created by the Creator, and when that one human being treats another human being a certain way, with difference, when you know we came from the same source, then it's like that person is not respecting the other's humanity (CC 1/3 12-2-93, 316–20).

The kindergarten teacher stated:

> People don't seek wisdom, and people don't seek the Creator for their direction . . . that's why I think so many things are out of balance in the world because they are not in tune with who created them or what we're supposed to be doing here on Earth (KT 2/5 10-14-93 44–47).

Additionally, principles of Native American pedagogy outlined in Chapter Two were used as pedagogical categories, and all interviews were searched and analyzed to document existence of such pedagogies (Appendix E). The Oneida role of the learner, or view of the child, was identified through the same process and is also reported in Appendix E.

Informant identifiers used during transcript analysis were: CC (Curriculum Coordinator)—the 47 year old Oneida Tribal School curriculum coordinator and Oneida culture expert; SA (Student Advocate)—a 61 year old Oneida woman who works as an advocate for Oneida children in a local public school. This woman is also the kindergarten teacher's mother; KT (kindergarten teacher)—the 33 year old participating teacher; E#1 (Elder #1)—an 82 year old woman elder and Oneida language instructor at the Oneida Tribal School; and E#2 (Elder #2)—an 86 year old man elder and Oneida language instructor at the Oneida Tribal school (Elders #1 and #2 are brother and sister). Throughout this manuscript, informants comments are coded in the following order; specific name, interview number, date of interview, and interviw lines. Example: Kindergarten teacher 2/5 10-14-93 34–42.

The Participating Teacher

Even a cursory viewing of Figure 1 reveals the participating teacher's central role in this study. Since determining the cultural appropriateness of Cognitively Guided Instruction for Indian children was a major purpose of the study, it was extremely important to select a culturally knowledgeable teacher. The kindergarten teacher, Ana, proved to be such a person. Born and reared on the Oneida Reservation, tribal school teachers and administrators identified Ana as a teacher sensitive to the cultural values of Oneida children and their families. Besides teaching kindergarten for three years, Ana also taught a culture course at a local junior college, assisted as a trainer/teacher specialist at the Children's Center, University of Wisconsin Green Bay for two years, and taught Headstart for six years.

During the Autumn of 1992, before she became comfortable with the content and routines of CGI, I frequently visited in Ana's classroom and observed teaching practices that reflected the tenets of Native American pedagogy as outlined in Chapter Two, and prior to participating in her initial CGI workshop, I asked her to write briefly about what she believed to be the teacher's role in mathematics instruction as well as the student's role. Her comments reflected beliefs that parallel Native American pedagogy (Appendix F). I also interviewed Ana in September 18, 1992. Analysis of the interview transcript revealed correspondence between her expressed beliefs and principles of Native American pedagogy. However, as discussed above, though Ana demonstrated in her instruction and verbalized in her interviews Native American cultural values, and though she taught an Oneida culture course at a local community college, she was unable to reflect on those values and correlate them with her own teaching. Hewson and Hollon (1994) reported a similar observation regarding teachers' inability to reflect on beliefs and practice:

> It would be nice if teachers could sit in silence, engage in self-analysis, and produce an objective picture of their beliefs

> about practice. But it's unlikely that self-reflection would reveal these relationships. Because most teachers work in isolation and have little help and incentive to engage in exploratory thinking and practices, like most of us, they find reflection on their assumptions difficult.

Not until Ana was asked to discuss Oneida values and to think about how those values influenced her instruction was she able to talk about an Indian way of teaching. The process of guided reflection gave Ana a conscious awareness of how her own cultural values influenced her.

Becoming a CGI Teacher

Ana's preparation to teach using the CGI approach extended over a two year period. During the summer of 1992, she participated in a five day, thirty hour, CGI workshop. Later, during the 1992–93 school year, she traveled to Madison, Wisconsin and spent a day visiting in classrooms of experienced CGI teachers. In the summer of 1993, she completed a second five day workshop, and in the spring of 1994, assisted me in presenting a workshop for teachers in a public school. However, at the completion of the study, Ana attributed my frequent visits to her classroom and our many CGI related conversations as of equal or more value than her workshop participation.

Documenting the Teacher's Beliefs about an Indian Way of Teaching and how CGI Corresponds with that Way

Having identified Oneida culture values, the second and third steps of the culture analysis process had to be completed: recognition and articulation of cultural beliefs held by the teacher and how those beliefs influenced her instruction as well as how they corresponded with Native American pedagogy, had to be documented. To accomplish this, five audiotaped and transcribed interviews were organized and analyzed according to the process described in the preceding section entitled, *Culture Interview Transcription and Analysis.* Additionally, how the teacher's cultural beliefs informed her mathematics instruction before CGI and after CGI, the teacher's beliefs about the cultural compatibility of CGI, and beliefs about how CGI influenced her students had to be explored. To do this, the same five audiotaped and transcribed interviews were analyzed and categorized, again through the process of repeated readings, according to four major topics:

1. The teacher's beliefs about the compatibility of CGI with Oneida/Native American culture;
2. The teacher's beliefs about how CGI influenced her students;
3. The teacher's beliefs about how CGI influenced her instruction; and
4. The teacher's personal feelings about mathematics before and after the CGI workshops and implementation experience (Appendix G).

Eight mathematics lessons were also recorded with detailed field notes, and four lessons were videotaped. Ana observed and commented on these videotaped lessons. Her comments regarding instructional decisions, culture, and students were transcribed and analyzed.

Student Performance

The ultimate test for determining the cultural compatibility of Cognitively Guided Instruction was evaluating how this approach influenced the mathematical problem solving ability of Oneida kindergarten children. Underlying the purpose of the study were two assumptions:

1. that mathematics taught in a culturally compatible way will positively influence the mathematical problem solving ability of Native American students; and
2. that Cognitively Guided Instruction is a culturally compatible approach to teaching mathematics to primary grade Native American students.

The process of validating these assumptions involved documenting the problem solving ability of Oneida kindergartners. Assessment of student performance and analysis of that performance followed the procedures of a highly credible and comprehensive Cognitively Guided Instruction kindergarten study completed in 1990 (Carpenter et al. 1993). This study was selected to serve as a measure of comparison because of its research credibility and the fact that the study documented the ability of kindergarten students to solve not only joining and separating problems but multi-step problems and multiplication and division problems as well. A description of the replication process follows.

Seventeen kindergarten students (nine boys and eight girls), all enrolled members of the Oneida Reservation, were observed throughout the school year and formally assessed in May. The average student age at fall enrollment was 5.4 years. All students were from the same classroom, and all students received mathematics instruction from the same teacher.

Solving of word problems played a prominent role in the mathematics instruction. The teacher presented the problems and provided the children with counters that they could use to solve the problems; however, the teacher avoided showing the children how to problem solve. Children regularly reported on their strategies for solving a given problem to the class. Most of the problem-solving experiences involved one-step word problems; however, two-step problems were introduced at the end of the school year. The teacher did attempt to adapt numbers in the problems to the counting skills of individual children, but numbers up to 25 were used by the end of the year for most of the children.

All students received parent consent (Appendix H) to participate in the study. The researcher interviewed each student individually in a room apart from the classroom. Each student was asked to solve the nine problems listed in Table 2. Each problem was read aloud to the child and reread as many times as the child requested. If the child asked for specific information from the question, the interviewer reread the entire sentence containing the information. Counters, paper, and pencil were available on the table, and each child was told that she or he could use any of those materials to help solve the problems.

All interviews were videotaped. If a child's solution was not readily understood, the child was asked to explain what she or he had done. The researcher coded each child's responses as each problem was solved. For each CGI problem type, there are a small number of easily identified solution strategies that children tend to use that provide the primary categories for coding. If a strategy did not conform to one of the typical characterizations, detailed notes were made about what the child had done. Responses were coded both in terms of the solution strategy used and whether the answer was correct (Appendix I). Only valid strategies were recorded in the Valid Strategies categories, but solutions that resulted in an incorrect answer due to a counting error were included in the Number Correct category. For a child's response to be coded as a valid strategy, the child had to use a strategy that would result in a correct answer if there was no counting error. However, the child had to complete the solution to the problem and report an answer that was off by no more than one or two. If a child started using an appropriate strategy but could not complete the problem, that strategy was not coded as a valid strategy. Therefore, the Valid Strategy category includes responses of children who correctly solved the problem plus responses of children who used a valid strategy but made a simple counting error.

The videotaped interviews of each child were observed two times by the researcher to evaluate the accuracy of the initial interview coding. Coding results were also checked for reliability following a random selection coding process. This process involved randomly selecting three videotaped interviews, coding of the interviews by a researcher (other than the author of this study), and comparing the coded evaluations to determine inter-rater agreement. Inter-rater coding resulted in 96% agreement.

Table 2: Interview Problems

Problem type	Order given	Problem
Simple Word Problems Separate (result unkown	**1**	Paco had 13 cookies. He at 6 of them. How many cookies does Paco have left?
Join (change Unknown)	**3**	Carla has 7 dollars. How many more dollars does she have to earn so that she will have 11 dollars to buy a puppy?
Compare	**5**	James has 12 balloons. Amy has 7 balloons. How many more balloons does James have than Amy?
Multiplication	**2**	Robin has 3 packages of gum. There are 6 pieces of gum in each package. How many pieces of gum does Robin have altogether?

Table 2 (cont.)

Problem type	Order given	Problem
Measurement division	**4**	Tad had 15 guppies that he put into jars. If he put 3 guppies in each jar. How many jars did Tad put guppies in?
Partitive	**6**	Mr. Gomez had 20 cupcakes. He put the division cupcakes into 4 boxes so that there were the same number of cupcakes in each box. How many cupcakes did Mr. Gomez put in each box?
Division with remainder	**7**	19 children are going to the circus. 5 children can ride in each car. How many cars will be needed to get all 19 children to the circus?
Multistep	**8**	Maggie had 3 packages of cupcakes. There were 4 cupcakes in each package. She ate 5 cupcakes. How many are left?
Nonroutine	**9**	19 children are taking a minibus to the zoo. They will have to sit either 2 or 3 to a seat. The bus has 7 seats. How many children will have to sit 3 to a seat, and how many will have to sit 2 to a seat?

Chapter 4

Findings

The findings reported in this chapter are sequenced according to three research themes addressed in the study: first, Oneida culture values that impact on Oneida instruction and the relationship of those values to Native American pedagogy are summarized; second, the kindergarten teacher's views regarding the cultural compatibility of CGI are presented; and finally, data reporting the problem solving abilities of seventeen Oneida kindergarten children are described. Several comments discussing how Native Americans view people who perceive themselves as experts are also presented. These comments relate directly to the unexpected problems, described in Chapter Three, of locating a study site and receiving permission to complete the study. How these comments relate to cultural pedagogy will be discussed in Chapter Five.

Summarizing findings about culture distilled from interviews and experiences situates the research in an interpretive paradigm. Since interpretation is a human act, avoiding bias is impossible. The use of multiple informant voices helped ground the selection of a specific cultural value, but the final decision as to which voiced belief or behavior to select and label as representative of a culture became the interpretive responsibility of the researcher. In an attempt to control biased selection, documents produced within the community (Appendix C) as well as personal observations of social interactions within the Oneida Tribal School were reflected on during the value selection process.

An additional paradigmatic aspect, one that has been alluded to throughout this study, needs to be considered before findings are reported, and that aspect is the fact that within the study community, the researcher is both an insider, the daughter of an Ojbwe Native American, and an outsider, an academic investigator. Narayan (1993) describes this duality as being minimally bicultural in terms of belonging simultaneously to the world of engaged scholarship and the world of lived experience. She supports this position and calls for *hybridity* of text:

> One wall stands between ourselves as interested readers of stories and as theory-driven professionals: another wall stands between narrative (associated with subjective knowledge) and analysis (associated with objective truths). By situating ourselves as subjects simultaneously touched by life-experience and swayed by professional concerns, we can acknowledge the hybrid and positioned nature of our identities. Writing texts that mix lively narrative and rigorous analysis involves enacting hybridity, regardless of our origins. (682)

The present chapter qualifies for the label of hybrid text. The selection of informant comments and the interpretations of those comments were influenced both by the researcher's inculcated Native American belief system and acculturated knowledge of ethnographic methodology.

Oneida Culture Values

During the two years that I spent working with teachers implementing CGI at the Oneida Tribal School, I heard teachers and school leaders speak often about the importance of giving thanks to the Creator, I stood reverently with the entire student body during tobacco burning ceremonies of thanksgiving on the school grounds, I read many references to the Creator on posters in the school hallways, I observed teachers burning cedar in classrooms to rid the rooms of bad spirits, and I was invited to participate in the mid-winter Peach Pit ceremony at the community Longhouse. These experiences led me to conclude that spirituality, the belief in the Creator, was an underlying value shared by many Oneida community members. This conclusion was not based solely on observations; it was affirmed by my personal belief in spirituality, a Creator-focused spirituality acquired in early childhood and retained as an adult.

Additionally, each Oneida document, selected with the help of an Oneida culture expert and used to stimulate discussion during culture value interviews, emphasized spirituality, and during the culture interviews, all five Oneida educators expressed belief in the Creator and the importance of spirituality. The following selection of interview comments reveals this shared foundational belief.

The Belief in the Creator

> The Creator gave away of himself to make things, to make the universe, the stars, the plants, to make all this [gestures outside the window] (Curriculum Coordinator 1/3 12-2-93, 19–21).
>
> He [the Indian] knows that he was born into spirituality, and if he chooses to use it, it just furthers his life (Student Advocate 1/1 11-18-93, 183–85).
>
> I try to teach them balance, that being Oneida doesn't make them better, it just makes them special to the Creator (Kindergarten Teacher 2/5 10-14-93, 38–41, page 7).
>
> All Indians have basically the same culture . . . who we say prayers to, who we give thanks to, and nature (82 Year Old Elder/Woman 1/1 11-2-93, 306–10).
>
> We give thanks to the Creator (86 Year Old Elder/Man 1/2, 11-21-93, 615–16).

Three additional values: the importance of harmony, the importance of generosity, and the importance of cooperation were also emphasized, but they were subsumed under the primary value of believing in the Creator and the giving act of creation.

The Importance of Harmony

> The Creator in his wisdom made polarities so that there would be constant movement, constant interchange. . . . What this leads us to is a philosophy of balance and harmony (Curriculum Coordinator 2/3 12-9-93, 34–60).

I think most Indians want harmony, seek harmony (Student Advocate 1/1 11-18-93, 338–39).

[The values that I would say are unique to Indian people are] teaching respect, teaching the children to get along with others, to be in balance with nature, to be in balance with themselves spiritually. . . . Native Americans believe in using the medicine wheel to find balance with your spirit—your mental, your physical, your social, your spiritual. When all of those things are in harmony, then you're at your best (Kindergarten Teacher 2/5, 10-14-93, 34–37 page 1).

The Importance of Generosity

The Creator was able to give of Himself, share of Himself, His basic energy. . . . That became the law. . . . So this give away continues. Otherwise life stops, ends. So we have ceremonies that promote giving (Curriculum Coordinator 1/3 12-2-93, 112–30).

When somebody needs something and we have it, we'll help. So, there goes whatever you've tried to save for a while. . . . Let them have it. We'll make some more another day. . . . It's an honor to do something for somebody else (Student Advocate 1/1, 12-18-93, 275–84, 365–66).

All the Indian people I know, like my family, they always put you before themselves. . . . When I think of my great-aunts or my grandmother [they] always wanted to meet your needs first. They always wanted to invite you in and feed you and clothe you. If you liked something, they would give it to you (Kindergarten Teacher 2/5 10-14-93, 48–55, p. 5).

[The Oneida] were never greedy. Even if you go back to the Revolutionary war. The Iroquois fed the United States army. They didn't say, "You owe us so much money." [It was a] Gift. They are not greedy. A true Oneida doesn't look for wealth (86 Year Old Elder Man 1/2 12-2-93, 540–42).

The Importance of Cooperation

> I think sharing was a concept that began in the beginning, but there are things that came after it to help maintain the concept. I would say that cooperation is that. There were guidelines and rules of behavior and rituals set up and community procedures set up that were cooperative and that helped ensure that sharing kept going on from the past to the present and to the future. So they were related that way (Curriculum Coordinator 1/3 12-2-93, 88–94).

> I would rather everybody shared in whatever achievement there is . . . I don't like to call attention to myself by doing something or having somebody recognize me . . . I am part of a whole family. I have never made decisions by myself (Student Advocate, 1/1 11-18-93, 284–86).

> I think the Oneidas are real strong in having a real democracy. Everybody contributes to the decision making, and that's the value system that I try to do in my classroom: that everyone has a part, which everyone has to contribute to the decisions that we make. We talk things out and everyone's opinion is shared in a talking circle (Kindergarten Teacher 2 /5 10-14-93, 37–42).

> Our idea is to cooperate, work together. Of course, half the time we don't do it, but that's what we try (82 Year Old Elder Woman 1/1 11-2-93, 353–54, 392–93).

Interconnectedness of all Values

In the following excerpt, the curriculum coordinator integrates the preceding values and concludes with comments pertaining to educating children for harmonious living.

> Indian people can never be part of the "I" generation. They can never be that because they carry this serious responsibility . . . the responsibility of understanding the life-giving forces that are at work, that everything is interconnected, that nothing can exist by itself, on its own, in isolation. This is how balance and harmony are achieved . . . in order to find harmony, there must be cooperation. The society must value the concept of cooperation in order for individuals

> to focus on their own unique roles. If everybody were to fulfill their responsibilities according to this belief system, harmony would be achieved on this planet. The fact is that we're not fulfilling our responsibilities. That's why there are so many problems in the world. The only way to get people to understand this goal is to begin in early childhood. That's the focus of all of our stories and legends. One of the key themes of American Indian stories is sharing, generosity, stinginess. We begin very simple and then as they mature lead them to higher levels of awareness. If people understand it, believe it, and really live it, act it, then we will have harmony (Curriculum Coordinator 3/3 5-18-94, 232–42, 318–37).

This comment communicates the spiritual-based philosophy that grounds Oneida education: everything on the planet was created to be interconnected—nothing can exist on its own, and an educational system that emphasizes the "I" of individualism will produce a planet of problems; harmony is achieved through cooperation; and, through cooperation, one identifies his/her unique role and gains autonomous responsibility.

The Oneida View of the Child

Situated within this philosophy is the belief that each child placed on this planet by the Creator is an innately capable being assigned a special mission in the interconnected schema of life. All informants expressed this belief and the influence of this belief is apparent in the curriculum coordinator's and kindergarten teacher's comments about the role of the learner:

> The child is definitely not considered a blank slate. As a matter of fact, a child is considered a gift or a prize to a family. We also have this belief in missions, that everyone has an individual mission. It might be something as simple as being a mom or being a good aunt to one or two people, or it could be a major mission. They are born with that mission, a good mission. You don't know what it is, so you give the little children room and space and respect because they, like yourself, have something to do in this life (Curriculum Coordinator, 1/3 12-2-93, 393–410).

> One of the things that's passed along through culture is the belief that what we do today is going to benefit or harm the next seven generations, and that is the Great Law. So we have to be mindful of how we are treating the kids. . . . I think every creation is special, and God gives you special gifts, and every child has strengths, and I think as teachers, you need to bring out those strengths and help that child feel confident about something that he or she can do the very best (Kindergarten Teacher 2/5, 10-14-93, 4-8 p2, 17–20 p3).

The Oneida Way of Teaching Children

All informants were asked to discuss their views on an ideal Oneida way of teaching children. They were also asked to review the five principles of Native American pedagogy outlined in Chapter Two and to comment on these principles. All informants stated that the generalized Native American principles corresponded with Oneida beliefs and should be recognized as principles of culture-based Oneida instruction. The kindergarten teacher's comments were representative of the other participant's but addressed instruction specifically:

Principle #1: Teacher as Facilitator: Indirect Rather than Direct Instruction

> I don't know everything. We are a body of learners together, and they (the students) can teach me things. I want them to feel that they are equal to me, that they can ask me anything, that they can be participants in their learning, that they can be involved in what's going on in our classroom. You find out their strengths by getting to know what they want to learn about and facilitating what needs to be learned that way. In a way, that's a real good balance, and with that the kids are happy with their learning balance (KT, 2/5 10-14-93, 38–49 p2).

The teacher's perception of her status as being equal to each student and her goal of facilitating learner strengths in order to achieve balance, fulfilled mission, reflects her spiritually grounded beliefs: belief in the Creator's ordained value of equality and belief in the importance of achieving balance or harmony through mission fulfillment.

Principle #2: Problem Solving that is Sense-making

> I think hands-on is easier, instructing them in that way so that they can do it themselves. I think that's traditionally how they did things . . . it was more of a hands-on approach (KT 2/5 10-14-93, 23–26, p9).
>
> I think that in the old way when a problem would arise it was looked at as something to learn from (KT 3/5 10-20-93, 255–56).

The researcher's interpretation of the teacher's comments for Principles #2 and #3 and their relationship to Oneida values will be discussed following Principle #3 comments.

Principle #3: Problems Based on the Lived Experiences of the Students and Culturally Contextualized

> Learning from daily experiences, that way you're taking from their lives something that's valid and turning that into something that helps them learn. I try to incorporate the culture and what we are working on and what's important to them. Like this year, I have a little boy in the classroom with leukemia. So we are trying to learn about cancer (KT 3/ 5 10-20-93, 244–50).

Instruction for pre-industrial Indian people focused on transmitting group values and resolving survival problems in balanced and harmonious ways, such as, harvesting only what was needed and not exhausting resources. Elders told stories and parents allocated tasks appropriate to children's capabilities, applied tasks that served the community. In contrast, today's programs of public education with printed texts and competitive industrialized management systems, stand as institutions of conflict for Native American learners, conflict influenced not only by differing values, i.e., cooperation rather than competition, but conflict related to learning experience. When cognition and learning is viewed through a historical lens, it is not surprising to learn that today's Indian children benefit most from instruction that encourages hands-on and applied problem solving.

Principle #4: Cooperative Rather than Competitive Instruction

> I try to use cooperative learning so that we're all learning together so that we all feel good about learning (KT 2/ 5 10-14-93, 4–17, p8).

> I think a teacher has to meet the individual needs. If they are a little bit further, then they have to be challenged, but my kids who are brighter help the other kids. We do that as cooperative learning, and we talk a lot about how some people are good at this, and others are better at something else, and that they are best at one thing. We just have to find it. I always plan my lessons so that everyone will have success and they'll feel good about sharing that. And we talk a lot about not embarrassing another person (KT 3/ 5 10-20-93, 59–68).

For Native American people, harmony is achieved through cooperation. Yet, this form of cooperation does not obliterate individualism. Rather, it identifies and esteems individuality through the concept of Creator ordained personal mission. To survive, a community relies on each member to fulfill her/his mission. One mission is not more important than another; being a good aunt is as important as being a good doctor in the circle of life. To the Creator, everyone is equal.

Principle #5: Time-generous Rather than Time-driven Instruction

> I think Indian people have their own time. I think that the learning process always continues. It is not like on a time thing, like you're supposed to learn this at this time, or you should know it by now, or like at one o'clock you should know everything, whatever the time is, that you should have all the answers for tests and stuff like that. I think that you are continually learning and adding to your base, and that's, I think, how I think Native American taught each other a long time ago (KT 2/5 10-14-93, 1–6 p10).

With industrialization came time cards, time management, the "time is money" value. Today, to most mainstream Americans, money means acquiring individual possessions, and for industrial barons, acquiring possessions means market demand and capital gain. A brief reflection on this scenario and its relationship to traditional Native American values reveals stark cultural conflict, and the comments expressed above document the abiding presence of this conflict.

The Native American Perspective on Authority Figures

Related to the view of the child discussed in the preceding section and Principle #1, Indirect rather than Direct Instruction , and Principle #2, Cooperation Rather than Competition, is the Indian view of individuals who claim to be authorities. Understanding this view also provides some insight into the problems of finding a study site and then receiving approval to complete this study.

> The authority figure that's where the cross-cultural conflict enters in. The authority figure comes in and the Indian evaluates that person . . . sizes that person up as having bad manners . . . that person must be wrapped up in himself. . . . When a new teacher comes in, if that young child was taught in the home how to regard humanity, that regard is given to the essence of who we are. When children see that lived in front of them: they see their parent's behavior, their older brother's and sister's behavior, they see how guests are treated, well, when they are in the classroom, they expect to be treated the same way. Now, I'm talking about a traditional Indian family. I know there are many cases where this isn't going on, and even in those cases, I think, to some degree, it's still there. I think in the classroom the children are kind of appalled when a non-Native teacher comes in and acts like an authority, acts like they know everything. Here's this young child of five, seven, or nine thinking this way, and they know culturally, in their own families that this would not be accepted. . . . Social status goes to people who can share and care the most. If a teacher wants to impress by throwing out vast knowledge that runs counter to what is good. So they look at a non-Native teacher behaving that way as being like a person who is almost sick. So right away, the children know they are in a situation where they are being dictated to, and they know that they have to follow through, behave, get the grades and do lots of other things, but it runs counter to their feelings inside about what is

> right. Some kids will play the game. Other kids will fight it tooth and nail. Others will pretend that they are going with the flow but aren't really. So they are not getting much out of the situation (Curriculum Coordinator 1/3 12-2-93, 309–68).

The Kindergarten Teacher's Views about CGI

A description of instruction and the teacher's views about the cultural compatibility of that instruction

Four kindergarten mathematics lessons were videotaped during the spring semester. On May 17th the teacher viewed two of these lessons, one based on a St. Patrick's Day theme and the other on a picture book, and identified examples of compatibility between CGI and Oneida culture-based pedagogy. The process of having the teacher view and discuss the videos was audiotaped, transcribed, and identified as interview #5. Below, the two selected lessons are briefly described and the interview transcripts discussing cultural pedagogy and CGI as identified by the teacher are reported.

Besides providing a resource to assist the teacher when reflecting on classroom practice, the video segments also served to validate that the teacher implemented CGI principles and knowledge in her instruction:

- the teacher did not show children how to solve problems, rather, students were encouraged to solve problems any way that made sense to them—in the instances reported below, the children used unifix cubes;
- the teacher selected problems based on what she knew her students were capable of accomplishing—careful observation of individual student solution strategies allowed the teacher to pose developmentally appropriate problems;
- the teacher varied the problems posed to students based on CGI knowledge of whole number problem types—students are asked to solve a partitive division problem, a join-result-unknown problem, etc.;
- students were encouraged to solve problems cooperatively;

- students were asked to explain their solution strategies to the teacher as well as to other students.

Though the behaviors reported here document that the teacher implemented CGI, it must not be assumed that she is a CGI "expert." The teacher identifies herself as a "becoming CGI teacher."
It is important to point out that though the lessons were *not* based on traditional Oneida culture themes (i.e., the Iroquois/Oneida game of lacrosse, the clan system, or beading), it was possible for the teacher to analyze the lessons and identify culturally responsive pedagogy; pedagogy can be cultural even if the topic of instruction doesn't appear to be. Furthermore, it is interesting to note that all of the kindergartners, all enrolled Oneida reservation members, wore green on St. Patrick's Day—though the lesson theme was not traditional Oneida, it was based on a shared contemporary experience of the students.

Video Segment #1: St. Patrick's Day Lesson

One of the St. Patrick's Day mathematics activities was that each child was to find three numbered paper shamrocks that had been hidden around the classroom. The purpose of the lesson was to give the students practice joining three numbers with combinations up to twenty-five. When the lesson began seventeen students were sitting in a semi-circle around the teacher listening to instructions.

Students were then dismissed five at a time to search for shamrocks. After finding three, each child went to his or her table area and started solving the problem using counters. One student's numbers were 7, 5, and 9. After making a set of 7 counters, then a set of 5 counters, then a set of 9 counters the child pushed the sets together and counted them all. The student wrote her answer on a small piece of paper, and then asked another student to check her answer by solving the same problem. All students followed the same routine as the teacher moved from student to student watching and asking children to explain what they were doing.

Teacher's Comments about Video Segment #1

Interviewer: Is there anything here that you would say is cultural?

Teacher: Just the fact that the kids are solving problems that they can succeed with. I'm not asking them to do something that they can't do. Some of them go on to different problems that are harder, but if someone isn't ready to do that, then they work with a problem that is right for them. I think that's being culturally sensitive. Relating it back to culture, children were given responsibilities and jobs that they were able to succeed at or were good at or they had the gifts to do. We believe that the Creator has given everyone some gift and everyone has different ways to do things. That way of teaching is culture, but it's also CGI because kids can solve problems in ways that make sense to them. There's not just one way.

Interviewer: I saw you ask students to work together to check each other's answers.

Teacher: In the culture, people work together. I think Indian people in general don't like to do things alone. Even me as an adult, I would rather work with someone else.

Video Segment #2: St. Patrick's Day Lesson Continued

The teacher sat at one large table where students were modeling solutions to word problems using counting cubes. She silently watched a girl solve a problem. When the student finished, she recorded her answer and showed it to the teacher. The child had miscounted one of the sets. The teacher asked the child to recount and patiently questioned the child until she had accurately counted the cubes.

Teacher's Comments about Video Segment #2

Interviewer: What was the value in asking her to explain all of that?

Teacher: I kept questioning her so she would check what she had done. This isn't a hard problem, and accuracy is what I wanted to work on.

Interviewer: What do you think questioning does for children's thinking?

Teacher: I think it helps them become better thinkers, also what I was doing was helping her become a more careful thinker. . . . I think the value in it is that the student gets a deeper understanding of what they are doing. Before, they would have a worksheet and would count the dots

> or whatever, but by thinking and talking about their thinking, it's like they get a deeper understanding. Talking about it affirms what has been done. Also, this kind of talking about the way a problem is solved helps show that there can be different ways of solving a problem. Before there was only one way. I think this is especially good for Native American students. They are more creative in their thinking. Sometimes I have a hard time understanding how they got their answers. They go in round about ways.

Video Segment #3: St. Patrick's Day Continued

At the end of the day, one last mathematics problem was given: If you had twelve pieces of gold and you wanted to share those pieces with three friends, how many pieces would each friend get? The students solved this problem individually while sitting on the floor in a semi-circle using counters. Students, after solving the problem, went to where the teacher was seated on the floor, and whispered their answers in her ear. One boy became frustrated (he has been adding 4 cubes and 3 cubes together) and began to cry. The teacher moved to him, put her arms around him, and said softly, "Just watch what Travis is doing."

Teacher's Comments about Video Segment #3

> Interviewer: How do you feel about kindergarten children doing division and multiplication problems?
>
> Teacher: They do okay. It's just beginning multiplication and division, but they can do it. This year's class took a longer time really understanding it, really enjoying it. Last year's group caught on more quickly, and they wanted challenging problems.
>
> Interviewer: Is it because they are less mature?
>
> Teacher: It's because I have such a wide range of ability. I can't move as quickly, but they're starting to enjoy those problems more.
>
> Interviewer: One thing that I have noticed about your teaching is that you move at a relaxed, steady pace. It's not rushed, and your voice is soft. How would you describe your style of teaching?

Teacher: Can I think about it [laugh, pause]? Well, first of all, I try to meet my students' needs depending on where they are. Like I said, that's culture. Then, I want to make learning enjoyable for them and fun. I try to give them all they need to feel good about learning. I guess that's my style. I believe that kids naturally learn on their own. A teacher just facilitates that learning by creating a good atmosphere. And I like to have the kids near me. Sometimes I think they are too far away from me when they are sitting in the circle. I like to have them come up close to me so I can see them and can make eye contact with them and make certain they are understanding.

Interviewer: I've noticed that you go to children. You don't call out to them.

Teacher: Ya, if they are having a hard time. Maybe that's my style. Maybe it's cultural. I remember my mom teaching me things, and she was always right next to me. She was always real close to me. Like when she wanted to show me something, she would always bring me close to her. She talked to me in a gentle voice. She never rushed. I feel that the reason I'm that way is because that's a carry-over from the way my mom treated me. Maybe that's culture. My mom's Oneida. Maybe it was just her gentleness, her spirit.

Interviewer: These are feelings that you held long before CGI.

Teacher: Right, but I think this style fits in a CGI classroom. In order to do CGI you have to be around the children, working with the children. You can't be sitting at your desk. You've got to be watching what they are doing. You have to be involved with what they are doing, and that means being right next to them. So if you have a problem being next to children, you might have a problem with CGI.

Interviewer: Ya, I agree. I believe that this is part of the correspondence between CGI and the traditional Indian way of teaching.

Teacher: And nurturing the child that's real cultural too. I feel that with CGI with every problem you give them, you're nurturing them to a higher level of thinking. You're nurturing their minds.

Interviewer: What is the Indian view of the child's mind?

Teacher: We believe that children are born with God given gifts that are to be nurtured as far as the child will go.

Video Segment #4: A Lesson on Sharing

After the morning calendar routine, the teacher read a book, *Rainbow Fish*, aloud. The theme of the story in this book was generosity. Throughout the day all content activities were integrated around the book: social studies, language arts, and math. Three math activities were dispersed throughout the day. Students solved three fish-related word problems, graphed sea creature crackers, and practiced addition of graphed groups with calculators.

At one point in the lesson, the teacher asked, "If we hold all of our goodness inside and don't share it with anybody, share our toys, our specialness, will we be happy?"

Teacher's Comments about Video Segment #4

Interviewer: What you said about sharing specialness, is that cultural?

Teacher: Oh yes. It can be traced back to creation.

Interviewer: What do you think is shared in CGI?

Teacher: In CGI children share their strategies, their thinking, but what is also shared is their enthusiasm, the eagerness to solve problems, and the satisfaction of success. You know, when a child says, "I got it!", when a child is really excited about solving a problem, that excitement is shared.

Interviewer: For Native American children, whether Navajo, Crow, Sioux, would you say that CGI is a culturally sensitive way of teaching mathematics for Indian children?

Teacher: You give the children the problem, it doesn't matter what tribe or color, and let the children work it out for themselves. This isn't anybody's way. This is the child's way, and I think it's the same with all children. With CGI, Native American children have the same

> opportunity as anybody. With CGI, children can makes sense in any way that their minds work, and they are given enough time to do it, and they can talk about it. That gives them success, and they feel good about math. So, for Indian children, I think CGI fits very well.

The classroom vignettes and transcribed comments presented above were selected to situate the teacher's thoughts regarding the cultural compatibility of Cognitively Guided Instruction within actual classroom practice. Careful reading of the comments confirms the teacher's belief in compatibility. In the next section, additional confirming evidence is presented.

Additional Interview Transcript Analysis

Four audiotaped and transcribed interviews were analyzed and categorized according to four topics:

1. The teacher's beliefs about the cultural compatibility of CGI,
2. The teacher's beliefs about how CGI influenced her students,
3. The teacher's beliefs about how CGI influenced her instruction, and
4. The teacher's feelings about mathematics before CGI and after CGI.

Complete tables displaying the findings of this analysis are presented in Appendix G. Below, selected comments communicate these findings.

Topic 1: The Teacher's Beliefs about the Cultural Compatibility of Cognitively Guided Instruction

> CGI would fit into a Native American style of teaching depending how in balance that person was with the culture. Ya, it would fit if you were a culturally balanced teacher (KT 4/5 4-14-94, 94–101).

> I guess why I want to do CGI math or why I'm involved with this research is because I value Indian children, and I know

> this way is right for them. I want them to be as successful as they can be. A lot of times they have to overcome such great obstacles just to be who they are and know who they are. So, by doing this, if I can help any other Indian child, it doesn't have to be Oneida, be better or find what they're best at, that's why I'm doing it (KT 2/5 10-14-93, 34–41).

Topic 2: The Teacher's Beliefs about how Cognitively Guided Instruction Influenced Her Students

> I see the kids how they are having fun. . . . They're talking a lot more. They always want to ask, "What's more?" now. With anything that we do, they are asking math questions. . . . I guess I feel that I underestimated them all this time because of all the developmental stuff that I've read, that they can only do this at this age, but they can do far more. They are very bright. . . . I look at them differently now. . . . The kids are noticing things more because they are talking about math so much. . . . I know that they are looking at their world in a different way (KT 1/5 9-18-92, 53, 221–27, 344–50, 580–87).

Topic 3: The Teacher's Beliefs about how Cognitively Guided Instruction Influenced Her Instruction

> (CGI) gives them the freedom to think, to problem solve for themselves and come up with answers that don't have to be right or wrong. . . . I tell them I'm concerned with what they think and how they did it. I say, "your friends are going to check your work. I don't know what's the right answer." We're on equal ground now because they know that I don't have all the right answers all the time, and I have to figure it out myself (KT 1/5 9-18-92, 412–21).

> This just seems more natural. I make lessons from what intrigues them. . . . I've incorporated my own ideas, and I'm not relying on a workbook (KT 1/5 9-18-92, 261–67, 519–21)

> Now I'm doing a lot more visual things like graphing, voting on things, then graphing and asking questions about the graph, having them compare, and now I use literature, integrate math into stories that I read aloud and then ask math questions from.

> I integrate the culture more. I ask math questions from culture stories (KT 4/5 4-14-94, 52–56).

Topic 4: The Teacher's Attitudes about Mathematics before and after Working with Cognitively Guided Instruction

> Personally, I never really liked math, but I'm learning to be more appreciative of it since CGI. Now it's a lot more fun, and I'm finding more ways to incorporate it into my classroom, and as I see the kids how they're having fun, it makes me want to challenge them more (KT 1/5 9-18-94, 48–54).

> (Why I like CGI is) everybody can feel successful. I can remember not being so successful in math. I still have a math phobia. So it's real uplifting and real nice to see these little kids enjoying math (KT 2/5 10-14-93, 30–36).

> I guess the biggest difference is now I have a better understanding of math and how kids develop, go through stages to get where they understand. I know when I used to teach math the kids couldn't get it. Now I realize that there are different stages, different developmental stages in problem solving, in how they understand. Now I know it's not the fault of the child. It's just that they are not at that level (KT 4/5 4-14-94, 31–38).

> I understand the problem types, and I'm beginning to understand the way kids go about solving them, their strategies. Before, I didn't know how to do that. I really didn't understand the developmental levels of children's thinking as far as math is concerned. I didn't even understand the math. I just followed the workbook manual and had the kids do what they were supposed to do in the workbook to cover that year, and I always wondered why kids were struggling.

To this point, the present chapter has focused on responding to research questions #1: What cultural values influence Oneida instruction, and do those values correspond with the values which underlie Native American pedagogy as outlined in the literature review? and research question #2: Did the participating kindergarten teacher believe that Cognitively Guided Instruction is a culturally compatible way of teaching mathematics to Oneida/Native American children? The next section responds to research question #3: How did Cognitively Guided Instruction influence the mathematical problem solving ability of the Oneida kindergarten students in this study?

The Problem-solving Ability of Oneida Kindergartners

The problem solving ability of the Oneida kindergartners was determined by analyzing their solution strategies to nine word problems (see Table 2, Page 46). Analysis revealed that the mathematical problem-solving performance of the 17 Oneida kindergartners in Ana's classroom when compared to the performance of a CGI study (N=70) completed in 1990 showed remarkable similarity. Eight of the Oneida children (47 % of the total compared to 46% in the 1990 study) used a valid strategy for all nine problems, although three of them made minor counting errors. Thirteen of the Oneida children (76% of the total compared to 63% in the 1990 study) used a valid strategy and correctly calculated the answer to seven or more problems. A summary of solution strategies is presented below, and performance percentiles for each of the nine problems are summarized in Table 3 at the end of the chapter. For a more detailed analysis of individual student performance see Appendix I.

Inter-rater reliability of the Oneida study followed a random selection process for coding agreement and resulted in 96% agreement.

Analysis of Oneida Kindergarten Solution Strategies

Separate (Result Unknown)

All seventeen children used a valid strategy for the separate (Result Unknown) problem. All seventeen children directly modeled the action in the problem by making a set of 13 counters, removing 6 of them, and counting the remaining counters.

Join (Change Unknown)

Thirteen children used a valid strategy for the Join (Change Unknown) problem. Nine children directly modeled the problem solution by making a set of 7 counters and adding on counters until there was a total of 11. Two children used a strategy that did not directly model the action in the problem. One child made a set of 11 counters and a set of 7 counters and then lined them up in one-to-one correspondence. The other child linked 11 counters together, recounted 7 of the counters, and then separated the 4 remaining counters. Two children counted up from 7 to 11.

Compare

Thirteen children used a valid strategy for the Compare problem. All thirteen directly modeled the problem by constructing the two distinct sets described in the problem, lining the two sets up in on-to-one correspondence, and counting the difference.

Multiplication

Sixteen children used a valid strategy for the multiplication problem. All sixteen children modeled the problem by making three sets with 6 counters in each set and then counting the three sets of 6.

Measurement Division

Thirteen children used a valid strategy for the Measurement Division problem. Eleven of the children first counted out a collection of 15 counters, put them in sets of 3, and counted the number of sets. Two children also made five sets of 3 counters each, but they did not initially count out 15 counters. Instead, they kept track of the total number of counters used as they constructed their sets. When they had counted out a total of 15 counters in groups of three, they counted the number of sets.

Partitive Division

Thirteen children used a valid strategy for the Partitive Division problem. All children directly modeled the problem making four sets with the same number of counters in each set to find the answer. There was two basic variation of this strategy. Three children systematically dealt the 20 counters one by one into four groups. Ten children made four groups of counters and adjusted the numbers in each group until the groups each contained the same number of counters and all of the counters were used up. Five of the ten children started out making four groups of 4 counters each and then added a counter to each group. The other five children used a variety of trial and error strategies to equalize the groups.

Division with Remainder

Twelve children used an appropriate strategy for the division problem in which they had to take into account that a whole car was needed to take care of the extra children. The problem is a measurement division problem, and they modeled it as such.

Multistep

Fourteen children used a valid strategy for the Multistep problem. All fourteen used counters to model the problem by making three groups of 4 counters and then removing 5 of the counters.

Nonroutine

For the problem in which 19 children had to be divided up 2 or 3 to a seat in a bus, responses were coded as correct if the children identified the number of seats that were occupied by two children and three children or if they identified the number of children who rode two to a seat and the number who rode three to a seat. Ten children used a valid strategy. Six children designated the seven seats with a counter and systematically dealt the 19 counters out into the seven groups. The other four children used trial and error to place the counters in seven groups containing either 2 or 3 counters.

Table 3: A Comparison of Percentiles of the Oneida study (N=17) and the 1990 Study (N=70).

Problem	**Oneida** %	**1990** %
Separate (Result Unknown)	100%	89%
Join (Change Unknown)	76%	80%
Compare	76%	71%
Multiplication	94%	86%
Measurement Division	76%	73%
Partitive Division	76%	70%
Division (Remainder)	71%	64%
Multistep	82%	67%
Nonroutine	59%	59%

Chapter 5

Discussion

Overview of the Chapter

Three questions focused this study:

1. What cultural values influence Oneida instruction, and do those values correspond with the values which underlie Native American pedagogy as outlined in the literature review?
2. Did the participating kindergarten teacher believe that Cognitively Guided Instruction is a culturally compatible way of teaching mathematics to Oneida/Native American children? If so, why?
3. How did Cognitively Guided Instruction influence the mathematical problem solving ability of the Oneida kindergarten students in this study?

The present chapter discusses these questions in four sections: the first two sections respond to questions one and two; the third section discusses question three; and the fourth section considers implications and draws conclusions.

Purpose of the Study

Completion of this study was motivated by the fact that Native Americans have the smallest percentage of secondary and post-secondary students performing at the advanced level in mathematics of all ethnic groups (Hillibrandt, Romano, Stang and Charleston 1992). The primary purpose of the study was to determine whether the teaching methods practiced by teachers implementing Cognitively Guided Instruction were compatible with the teaching methods of Native American pedagogy.

Two hypotheses grounded the study:

1. That Native American children who are taught with culturally sensitive methods of instruction will perform more successfully on mathematical problem-solving tasks; and
2. That Cognitively Guided Instruction, an approach that provides teachers with research-based knowledge about primary mathematics in relation to children's thinking, enables teacher's to construct ways of teaching that are compatible with Native American pedagogy.

These hypotheses can be combined into a simple syllogism: Native American children learn mathematics more successfully through culturally compatible methods of instruction; therefore, if Cognitively Guided Instruction shares ways of teaching that correspond with Native American methods of instruction, then Native American children who are taught with Cognitively Guided Instruction will experience mathematical problem solving success.

Determining the Cultural Compatibility of CGI

The initial step in determining the validity of the preceding syllogism was to identify pedagogies valued by Native American educators and then to compare those pedagogies to the teaching methods commonly practiced in CGI classrooms. The literature review reported in Chapter Two outlined five instructional methods that literature suggests are common across Native American tribes: indirect rather than direct instruction, problem solving based on sense-making, problem solving that is culturally situated and based on the lived experiences of the student, cooperative rather than competitive instruction, and time-generous rather than time-driven problem solving. These teaching methods were compared to those of teachers implementing Cognitively Guided Instruction, and it was determined that all five methods were methods commonly practiced by expert CGI teachers (Carey et al. 1994). Consequently, the proposal that Cognitively Guided Instruction is compatible with Native American methods of instruction was partially substantiated.

A major concern at this point in the study was that the five Native American pedagogies were idealized methods but not practiced when situated within any particular tribe. Determining common practice within a specific tribe had to be confirmed before compatibility of CGI could begin to be generalized. Testing the assumption required actual classroom experience. One Oneida Indian kindergarten teacher and her class of seventeen Oneida children were observed and interviewed in this study. Over a two year period, the teacher, an enrolled member of the Oneida reservation, willingly participated in two thirty hour CGI workshops, observed in CGI classrooms, and frequently conferenced with the researcher about CGI principles while implementing the approach in her classroom.

One would assume this teacher to be an informant capable of identifying commonalties and differences between a Native American way of teaching and Cognitively Guided Instruction. But this assumption was found to be invalid—the teacher was initially unable to articulate what a Native American way of teaching, more specifically, what an Oneida way of teaching might be. She possessed what Watson (1974) alluded to as "assumptions of everyday life . . . which are so much a part of the culture that they are not even consciously held." The kindergarten teacher had never been asked to reflect on what an Oneida way of teaching might be, and when asked to do this, her response was, "I really don't know."

Investigating the Deep Cultural Values that Influence Traditional Oneida Instruction

The teacher's initial inability to consider what an Oneida Indian way of teaching would be shifted the study from simply identifying common methods, such as indirect instruction and cooperative learning, to investigating the deeply held cultural beliefs that informed the teacher's instructional practices. Culture probing interviews with the kindergarten teacher as well as with four Oneida educators identified one unifying belief: the belief in spirituality and the divine act of creation, and three related values: valuing harmony, valuing generosity, and valuing cooperation. Each informant linked instructional practices such as cooperative grouping, indirect instruction, even trusting the child's ability to independently problem solve back to the Creator's intended purpose of placing life on the planet. The following comment by the Oneida Tribal School's curriculum coordinator expresses these beliefs.

> The universal truth being that life-producing, life-making is a give-away and a sharing, and we are exemplifying the Creator who did that first when creating and who gave the original instructions that this must continue . . . The importance of generosity and the importance of cooperation as a human phenomenon allows humans to replicate what is already surrounding us in nature. These behaviors help us fit into the interconnected schema. . . . If we don't, things will go out of balance. There will not be harmony. (CC 3/3 5-18-94, 107–50)

Interestingly, not until informal discussions with the kindergarten teacher reached this level of culture analysis was she able to reflect on her instructional practices and identify how her values and beliefs informed her teaching. Furthermore, not until she had reflected in this manner was she able to discuss her own Oneida way of teaching as well as the generalized Native American pedagogies outlined in the literature review. Only after such reflection was the teacher able to state that she believed the pedagogies were the same.

Besides enabling the teacher to consider the correspondence between her Oneida way of teaching and generalized Native American pedagogies, culture probing interviews also enabled the teacher to reflect on the teaching practices of Cognitively Guided Instruction and discuss how they corresponded with culturally informed methods of instruction. The following comments, selected from data presented in Chapter Four, were made during the fifth and final interview. During this interview, the teacher watched a videotape of her classroom instruction and commented on the cultural influences of her teaching decisions as well as how those decisions corresponded to Cognitively Guided Instruction.

> [With CGI] kids are solving problems that they can succeed with. I'm not asking them to do something that they can't do. Some of them go on to different problems that are harder, but

> if someone isn't ready to do that, then they work with a problem that is right for them. I think that's being culturally sensitive. Relating it back to culture, children were given responsibilities and jobs that they were able to succeed at or were good at or they had the gifts to do. We believe that the Creator has given everyone some gift and everyone has different ways to do things. That way of teaching is culture, but it's also CGI because kids can solve problems in ways that make sense to them. There's not just one way. (KT 5/5 5-17-94, 475–88)

> [Sharing is cultural.] It can be traced back to creation, and in CGI children share their strategies, their thinking, but what is also shared is their enthusiasm, the eagerness to share problems, and the satisfaction of success. You know, when a child says, "I got it!" When a child is really excited about solving a problem, that excitement is shared. (KT 5/5 5-17-94, 706–813)

> I think (CGI is culturally sensitive) because it's their own thinking. I don't want to say it's not white, that it's not a white man's way of thinking. You give the children the problem. It doesn't matter what tribe or color, and let the children work it out for themselves. This isn't anybody's way. This is the child's way, and I think it's the same with all children, that's the way God made them. With CGI, Native American children have the same chance as anybody. I think society at times has suppressed Indian people. I remember when I was going to school, I didn't think I was smart because I couldn't solve the problems the way I was supposed to, the way the book said. But with CGI, children can make sense any way that their minds work, and they are given enough time to do it. That gives them success, and they feel good about math. So, for Indian children, I think CGI fits very well. (KT 5/5 5-17-94, 719–36)

In these quotations, references to the deeply held cultural belief of spirituality are directly stated. However, throughout the study, unspoken spiritual values subtly influenced social interactions and even threatened to create misunderstandings. Examples include:

- the mathematics perspective held by a 61 year old Oneida school teacher, a perspective that associated mathematics with a greedy acquisition of wealth.
- the tribal school administrators who questioned my research intentions.
- the hesitancy of the tribal school board to grant permission for me to complete my study at the Oneida Tribal School.

These experiences must not be dismissed as interesting narratives incidental to the present study. Rather, each must be reflected on as culturally illuminating. Consideration of these experiences merely at a surface level might lead one to assume that the teacher held a narrow view of mathematics or that the tribal school leaders were unappreciative of unsolicited efforts and inconsiderate or even resentful when interacting with a researcher. Analysis at a deep culture level reveals the Native American value of generosity: generosity of material acquisitions for the benefit of the family and generosity of one's time given freely for the benefit of the community. The hesitancy on the part of the board members in granting research consent can be analyzed further at both levels: the surface level is obvious, the history of Indian exploitation by missionaries, educators, and anthropologists is well documented. Understanding the hesitancy from a deep culture level is best explained by the Oneida Tribal School curriculum coordinator:

> The authority figure—that's where the cross-cultural conflict enters in. The authority figure comes in and the Indian evaluates that person, sizes that person up as having bad manners, they see that that person must be so wrapped up in himself. He doesn't understand that he was created like everyone else. That person doesn't really want to help others. He wants to make himself look important. (CC 1/3 12-2-93, 309–23)

School board approval to complete this study was given only after I demonstrated that my intentions were to benefit Indian children, that they were not self-serving. The final sentence of a request for approval letter submitted to the school board by the curriculum coordinator stated, "Judy Hankes has given freely of her time."

I have chosen to report these culture-influenced interactions within this section to validate the point that the deeply held value of spirituality and the related values of generosity, cooperation, and harmony, permeated not only the instruction of the Oneida teacher but the patterns of communication within the general Oneida community, the community in which the teacher was enculturated.

Knowledge of the teacher's socially constructed and deeply held culture-based beliefs must be taken into consideration when reflecting on her confirmation of the cultural compatibility between her Oneida/Native American way of teaching and the instructional practices advanced by the users and developers of Cognitively Guided Instruction. Analysis of the derivations of the beliefs and values that underlie these compatible practices reveal that they differ drastically. As discussed above, Oneida/Native American pedagogy derived from the deeply held spiritual values of Indian people; whereas, the principles of Cognitively Guided Instruction derived from the integration of research-based knowledge constructed by educators within an academic community: one believes that the learner is capable of independent problem solving because that is what humans are created to do; the other believes that the learner is capable of independent problem solving because that is how human beings construct understanding.

How CGI Enhances Oneida/Native American Pedagogy

The preceding comments related to the compatibility of the Oneida/Native American way of teaching and CGI were taken from the final teacher interview. Related comments selected from the analysis of four earlier interviews are identified by topic and presented below. Complete tables displaying the findings of this analysis are presented in Appendix G.

Topic 1: The Teacher's Beliefs about the Cultural Compatibility of CGI

> I think it fits culturally just for the fact that with CGI it's more age appropriate. In the culture, they used to teach when children were ready, and I think that parallels. . . . The situation where the teacher is guiding them, not telling them,

where the teacher is letting them find their own answers, letting them draw conclusions for themselves. Also, I think there's more cooperation, more of a group effort. Everybody is encouraged to work together. It's not like they are trying to decide who is the best or who is not the best. It's where they are that's important and what they can contribute to the group. That's culture, and I see that in CGI. (KT 4/5 4-14-94, 7–12)

Topic 2: The Teacher's Beliefs about how CGI Influenced Her Students

They are happy to engage in math problems. It's not like there is pressure that they have to have the right answer or get the page done. They're excited about what they are doing. Kids are working solving problems because they want to. (KT 4/5 4-14-94, 115–27).

Topic 3: The Teacher's Beliefs about how CGI Influenced Her Teaching

It seems that I'm always doing math [laugh]. Before, I always had a set time. I took about 35 minutes to present, and then we did our little worksheets, but now we just to a lot more. . . it's more intertwined in everything that we do. (KT 1/5 4-14-94, 289–302)

I guess the biggest difference is I have a better understanding of math and how kids develop, go through stages to get where they understand. I know when I used to teach math, the kids just couldn't get it. Now I realize that there are different developmental stages in problem solving, in how they understand. Now I know it's not the fault of the child. It's just that they are not at that level. (KT 4/5 4-14-94, 31–38)

I really didn't understand the developmental levels of children's thinking as far as math is concerned. I didn't even understand the math. (KT 4/5 4-14-94, 70–80)

Topic 4: The Teacher's Attitudes about Mathematics before and after CGI

I think that as a Native American person, I think a lot of Native American people are like this, math wasn't something I

> liked in school. . . . I never grew up with a real confidence in math, so I guess a big thing that has changed for me is that now I feel more confident. (KT 4/5 4-14-94, 110–12, 131–33)

Developing Culturally Informed Mathematics Instruction

The comments reported in Topics 1 and 2 serve to affirm research question two, Is Cognitively Guided Instruction a culturally appropriate way of teaching mathematics to Oneida children? Here the teacher speaks about instructional compatibility as well as the mathematical problem solving success of her students. However, the interview analysis identified an aspect of Cognitively Guided Instruction that has received very little consideration within this study, and that is, How did this cognitive-based approach influence the teacher's instruction as well as her attitude about mathematics?

An interesting contradiction emerges at this point: if the methods of instruction of an Oneida/Native American way of teaching and Cognitively Guided Instruction share pedagogical principles, why, prior to CGI, did the teacher rely on a teacher's manual to inform her mathematics instruction, and, even though she was aware of the fact that her students were confused and unsuccessful when completing workbook pages, why did she continue with that instructional approach—especially when she was able to apply what has been identified as Oneida pedagogy when teaching other content areas? Two statements sequestered within the first selection of comments reported in Topic 3 answer these questions: "I really didn't understand children's developmental levels of thinking as far as math is concerned. I didn't even understand the math."

This dilemma was briefly discussed in Chapter Two, and an analogy was made between the abilities of a traditional storyteller and a CGI teacher: the storyteller has the knowledge of a story as well as sensitivity to the maturity of each listener—integration of this knowledge allows the storyteller to adjust the story for the audience; the CGI teacher has the knowledge of mathematics as well as the knowledge of children's thinking about mathematics—integration of this knowledge allows the teacher to pose problems according to the understanding of each problem solver.

The present study proposes that a third type of knowledge is important, the knowledge of value-based cultural pedagogy. However, though the study teacher possessed Oneida culture knowledge, her lack of mathematical knowledge and knowledge of children's thinking about mathematics forced her to compromise her cultural pedagogy and rely on culturally insensitive textbook instruction. The way she taught replicated the way she had been taught, and, having never developed mathematical understanding, she lacked the necessary knowledge to teach mathematics differently. Though she was an Oneida tribal member and culture expert, she was unable to teach mathematics in a culturally sensitive way.

The following diagram represents the crucial integration of the knowledge of cultural pedagogy with content knowledge and knowledge of children's thinking in the production of culturally informed or responsive mathematics instruction.

Figure 3

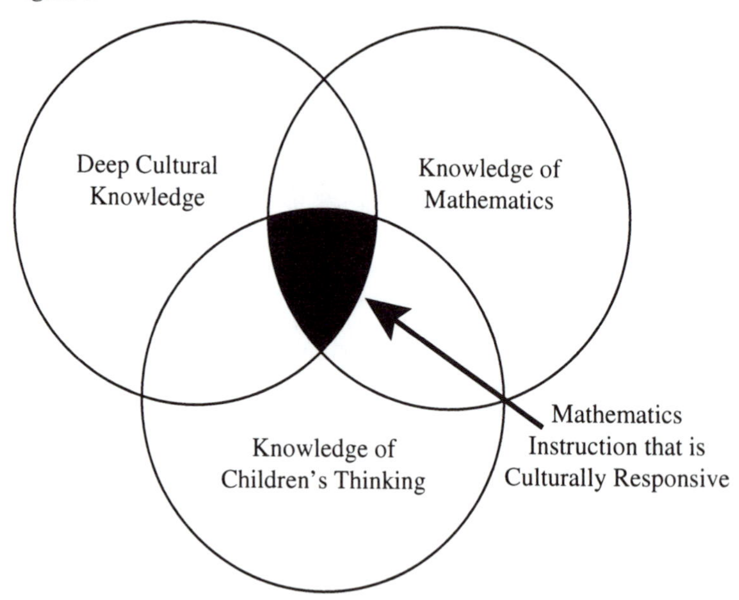

Mathematics Instruction that is Culturally Responsive

The deep culture knowledge referenced in this diagram is that latent socially-constructed and community-based knowledge that is integral to each person's life but difficult to articulate. It was this knowledge that the teacher had to become conscious of through thoughtful reflection before she was able to consider the cultural compatibility of Cognitively Guided Instruction. Additionally, the teacher had to become knowledgeable about Cognitively Guided Instruction, specifically the mathematics content and children's thinking about that content, before she was able to rely on this knowledge to inform her instruction and before she could recognize how processing this knowledge allowed her to teach in a culturally responsive way. The following comments reveal how this integrated knowledge influenced the teacher's instruction and mathematical confidence:

> My aide is, I think she is in shock because she just doesn't know where I'm coming from with all this stuff. Math ideas are just in my head now. They just come out when I'm thinking about CGI, thinking about ways of doing it, and math is fun for them now. . . . I never grew up with a real confidence in math, so I guess the big thing that changed for me is that now I feel more confident (KT 1/5 9-14-92, 475–85).

Problem Solving Success of Oneida Kindergartners Taught with CGI

The student problem-solving assessment procedures followed in this investigation replicated a Cognitively Guided Instruction kindergarten study completed in 1990 (Carpenter et al., 1993). A review of that study is presented here to provide background for understanding the Oneida kindergartners' performance.

The earlier study involved 70 children selected from six kindergarten classrooms in two schools. The schools were urban and served a diverse population. The specific purpose of the study was to investigate the solution processes of kindergarten children solving multiplication and division problems. Earlier studies documented that even before receiving instruction young children are able to solve a variety of different types of addition and subtraction word problems (Carpenter 1985; Fuson 1992). Other studies suggested that multiplication and division problems were more complex than basic addition and subtraction and inappropriate for kindergarten age children (Greer 1992; Kouba 1989; Schwartz 1988; and Vergnaud 1983). The findings of the 1990 study indicated that when kindergartners were allowed to solve multiplication and division problems intuitively by concretely modeling what the problem was asking them to do, they were successful.

Interestingly, the kindergartners in the 1990 study were more successful solving multiplication and division problems without instruction than first grade students and about as successful as third grade students who had received instruction, though the third graders used more sophisticated strategies (Kouba 1989). Additionally, the findings showed that the kindergartners were more successful in solving a division problem with a remainder (problem #7, Table 1) than were 13 year-olds asked to solve a similar problem in the 1983 National Assessment. The 1990 study implied that an emphasis on procedural computation had caused the older students to lose their intuitive problem solving ability. A conclusion drawn from the study was:

> If from an early age children are taught to approach problem solving as an effort to make sense out of problem situations, they may come to believe that learning and doing mathematics involves the solution of problems in ways that always makes sense (439).

As explained above, the Oneida assessment process replicated the 1990 study. Data analysis of the present study reveals that the Oneida kindergartners demonstrated similar performance when compared to the kindergartners in the 1990 study: on a nine item test (Table 2) the Oneida students performed as well as the 1990 kindergartners on one item, not as well on one item, and slightly better on seven items (Table 3). Additionally, of the 17 children tested in the Oneida study, eight used a valid strategy for all nine problems (47% of the total compared to 46% in the earlier study, and thirteen used a valid strategy and correctly calculated the answers to seven or more problems (76% of the total compared to 63% in the 1990 study). See Appendix I for analysis of each student's performance.

At this point, having compared the data of the two kindergarten populations, and having noted the somewhat higher performance of the Oneida students, it is fair to explain that the four teachers in the 1990 study were part of a cutting edge team investigating kindergartner's ability to solve multiplication and division problems. It was not without uncertainty that, toward the end of the school year, they introduced these problem types to their students. The findings of this earlier study were shared during the 1992 Cognitively Guided Instruction workshop in which the Oneida teacher participated. This research-based knowledge informed the Oneida teacher's instruction. Consequently, she introduced multiplication and division problem types earlier in the year. This information must be taken into consideration when comparing the performance of the kindergartners in the two studies. However, the fact remains that the Oneida children demonstrated remarkable mathematical problem-solving ability, an ability that contradicts assumptions of low mathematical aptitude among Indian children.

Implications

> Native American children learn mathematics more successfully through culturally compatible methods of instruction; therefore, if Cognitively Guided Instruction shares ways of teaching that correspond with Native American methods of instruction, then Native American children taught with Cognitively Guided Instruction will experience mathematical problem solving success.

Study findings suggest that this deductive argument is valid: Oneida culture-based teaching methods correspond with generalized Native American pedagogy; teaching methods of Native American pedagogy correspond with those of teachers implementing Cognitively Guided Instruction; and Oneida kindergartners taught with Cognitively Guided Instruction demonstrate mathematical problem-solving success. Having reported this conclusion, discussion of the study could end; however, an important aspect of Cognitively Guided Instruction needs to be considered. The fact that the Oneida students' performance closely replicated the performance of non-Indian kindergartners, and the findings of other studies which concluded that Cognitively Guided Instruction is highly successful for developing number sense with African American children (Carey 1993) and Hispanic children (Villasenor 1992) children, suggests one of two possibilities, either Cognitively Guided Instruction is a culture-free approach to teaching mathematics and appropriate for all cultures, or the classroom cultures of the non-Oneida Cognitively Guided Instruction studies shared values that correspond with those of the Oneida study. I resolve this quandary by proposing that respecting autonomy is a value shared by the developers and successful implementers of CGI as well as Native Americans. Autonomy has been documented as a Native American value for centuries (Erickson and Mohatt 1988; Hallowell 1955;

Kinietz 1972). To document that this value is also shared by the developers of Cognitively Guided Instruction, one needs merely to reflect on the principles of instruction advanced by this approach: in CGI classrooms children have the opportunity to engage in problem solving, discuss their solution strategies, and build on their own informal strategies for solving problems (Carey and Franke 1993). Though the reasons for valuing autonomy held by Native Americans and CGI researchers may differ, the value is shared and manifests itself through corresponding instructional principles.

Continuing with this line of reasoning, since all cultures do not value autonomy, it must be concluded that Cognitively Guided Instruction is not a culture-free approach for teaching mathematics. Teachers and students in an autocratic and highly competitive culture might find Cognitively Guided Instruction very frustrating. It is possible that, since Cognitively Guided Instruction is based on human learning theory, the approach is appropriate for all learners but not compatible with all cultures. Research is needed to investigate this supposition.

Conclusion

It is believed that the present study provides convincing evidence that one Oneida kindergarten teacher affirmed Cognitively Guided Instruction to be a culturally compatible way of teaching mathematics to Native American children and that seventeen Oneida kindergartners taught with this approach demonstrated mathematical problem solving success. Further research is needed to determine its effectiveness at other primary grade levels as well as with other Native American populations.

Background Information

I feel it is important to credit "akyot^hsla" (Oneida word for destiny or mission) with the fact that my dissertation study is about primary level mathematics instruction for Indian children. I found myself working for the Cognitively Guided Instruction (CGI) project not entirely by choice but consequential to receiving an Advanced Opportunity Fellowship, a fellowship granted because my father is Ojbwe. The fact is I chaffed at accepting such a fellowship, at being considered a token Indian in a mathematics education department.

However, circumstances and finances forced me to not only accept the fellowship but also to face a major obstacle—petrifying mathematics anxiety. I had become convinced that I was mathematically incompetent during high school.

Three things gave me the confidence to overcome this anxiety: many years of experience teaching in a primary classroom, the fact that CGI is based on cognitive learning theory, and the belief that CGI principles are compatible with American Indian values of cooperation and community building. The more I read about CGI and participated in discussions with project researchers, the more convinced I became of its cultural appropriateness for Indian children.

In some strange way, a way that I choose not to analyze or attempt to explain, completion of this study was also influenced by crows, the large black birds that many look upon with disdain. Throughout the study crows encouraged me, kept me on task. In Chapter Three I described how four crows communicated a sense of assurance that permission would be granted for completion of my study at the Oneida Tribal School. After that experience, crows continued to support my work. Even this morning, as they have each morning since April, loud cawing voices outside my window awakened me and urged me to continue writing.

Almost all Native American tribes tell legends about crows and ravens. One story that I heard long ago, I cannot attribute it to any particular tribe, describes the crow as a trickster capable of slipping incognito into a neighboring camp. Once in the camp, this trickster spies out information, learns new ways, and then returns to its own camp and reports. In this legend the crow is bicultural, able to shift between camps/cultures without losing its identity and loyalty.

In early April, a pair of crows started building a nest in the top of a spruce tree in my backyard. Often, the pair sat in a pine tree outside the window where I worked at my laptop computer. I watched them select and break off dead branches for their nest and listened to their soft clucking conversations. While watching this pair, I thought about the bicultural crow legend and came to identify with that crow shifting between communities, about myself shifting between the academic and the Indian cultures. I also thought about Cognitively Guided Instruction benefiting Indian children.

Interestingly, that same April, a pair of crows nested in the top of a tall spruce tree outside the fourth floor window of the university mathematics education department. Many people stopped by to look into the large, coarse nest. There were conversations about how ugly the babies were, about how the mother sheltered them when a heavy late spring snow blanketed the campus, about crows in general. But for me, the strategic location of the nest, outside the department window, reminded me of the exclusion of Indian people from mathematics discourse.

In May a young crow, having fallen out of the backyard nest, was rescued by my husband from the mouth of our large chow dog. By all rights it should have died, but it didn't. It wasn't supposed to. It's as though it wasn't enough that crows were to inspire from a distance, one had to participate in the very act of typing this dissertation. We called the fledgling Crow, and in the photo below Crow sits on my printer and watches me type.

Occasionally s/he would jump onto the keyboard, scrambling nonsense words into the text. When this happened, I carefully studied what was written, thinking perhaps there was a message—who knows—but there never was. Crow stayed with us into the summer and then learned to fly, to roost outside. Early in the morning I would stand on the back porch and call, "Crow! Crow!" S/he would caw from a nearby treetop, and a fluttering of large black feathers would carry this winged spirit to my wrist. Then in the middle of the night, I heard Crow cry out in fright; in the morning s/he was not there, and I was reminded of the dangers one encounters while living in a bicultural world.

Appendix A

Cognitively Guided Instruction Problem Types And Solution Strategies

Table 1: Classification of Word Problems

Problem Type		Addition and Subtraction	
I. Join	A. Connie had 5 marbles. Jim gave her 8 more marbles. How many does Connie have altogether? (result unknown)	B. Connie has 5 marbles. How many more marbles does she need to win to have 13 marbles altogether? (change unknown)	C. Connie had some marbles. Jim gave her 5 more marbles. Now she has 13 marbles. How many marbles did Connie have to start with? (start unkown)
II. Separate	A. Connie had 13 marbles. She gave 5 marbles to Jim. How many marbles does she have left? (result unkown)	B. Connie had 13 marbles. She gave some to Jim. Now she has 5 marbles. How many did Connie give to Jim? (change unkown)	C. Connie had some marbles she gave 5 to Jim. Now she has 8 marbles left. How many marbles did Connie have to start with? (start unkown)

Table 1 (cont.)

III. Part-Part-Whole	A. Connie has 5 red marbles and 8 blue marbles. How many marbles does she have?	B. Connie has 13 marbles. Five are red and the rest are blue. How many blue marbles does Connie have?	
IV. Compare	A. Connie has 13 marbles. Jim has 5 marbles. How many more marbles does Connie have than Jim?	B. Jim has 5 marbles. Connie has 8 more than Jim. How many marbles does Connie have?	C. Connie has 13 marbles. She has 5 more marbles than Jim. How many marbles does Jim have?

Table 2: Multiplication, Measurement Division, and Partitive Division Problems

Multiplication	Megan has 5 bags of cookies. There are 3 cookies in each bag. How many cookies does Megan have altogether?
Measurement Division	Megan has 15 cookies. She puts 3 cookies in each bag. How many bags can she fill?
Parititive Division	Megan has 15 cookies. She put the cookies into 5 bags with the same number of cookies in each bag. How many cookies are in each bag?
Source: Carpenter, T. P., Fennema, E. & Franke, M. L. (1994). Cognitively guided instruction: Children's thinking about whole numbers. Madison, WI: Wisconsin Center for Education Research.	

Table 3: Children's Solution Strategies

Direct Modeling Strategies	
Strategy	Description
Joining All Ellen had 3 tomatoes. She picked 5 more tomatoes. How many tomatoes does Ellen have now?	Using objects or fingers, a set of 3 objects and a set of 5 objects are constructed. The sets are joined and the union of the two sets is counted.
Separating From There were 8 seals playing. Three seals swam away. How many seals were still playing?	Using objects or fingers, a set of 8 objects is constructed. 3 objects are removed. The answer is the number of remaining objects
Separating To There were 8 people on the bus. Some people got off. Now there are 3 people on the bus. How many people got off the bus?	A set of 8 objects is counted out. Objects are removed from it until the number of objects remaining is equal to 3. The answer is the number of objects removed.
Joining To Chuck had 3 peanuts. Clara gave him some more peanuts. Now Chuck has 8 peanuts. How many peanuts did Clara give him?	A set of 3 objects is constructed. Objects are added to this set until there is a total of 8 objects. The answer is found by counting the number of objects added.
Matching Megan has 3 stickers. Randy has 8 stickers. How many more stickers does Randy have than Megan?	A set of 3 objects and a set of 8 objects are matched one-to-one until one set is used up. The answer is the number of objects remaining in the unmatched set.
Trial and Error Deborah had some books. She went to the library and 3 more books. Now she has 8 books altogether. How many books did she have to start with?	A set of objects is constructed. A set of 3 objects is added to or removed, and the resulting set is counted. If the final count is 8, then the number of elements in the initial set is the answer. If it is not 8, a different initial set is tried.

Table 3 (cont.)

Counting Strategies	
Strategy	Description
Counting On From First Ellen had 3 tomatoes. She picked 5 more tomatoes. How many tomatoes does she have now?	The counting sequence begins with 3 and continues on 5 counts. The answer is the last term in the counting sequence.
Counting on From Larger Ellen had 3 tomatoes. She picked 5 more tomatoes. How many tomatoes does she have now?	The counting sequence begins with 5 and continues on 3 counts. The answer is the last term in the counting sequence
Counting Down There were 8 seals playing. Three seals swam away. How many seals were still playing?	A backward counting sequence is initiated from 8. The sequence continues for 3 counts. The last number in the counting sequence is the answer.
Counting Down To There were 8 people on the bus. Some people got off. Now there are 3 people on the bus. How many people got off the bus?	A backward counting sequence starts from 8 and continues until 3 is reached. The answer is the number of words in the counting sequence.
Counting On To Chuck had 3 peanuts. Clara gave him some more peanuts. Now Chuck has 8 peanuts. How many peanuts did Clara give to him?	A forward counting sequence starts from 3 and continues until 8 is reached. The answer is the number of counting words in the sequence.
Deriving and Fact Recall Strategies	
Strategy	Description
Deriving Six frogs were sitting on lily pads. Eight more frogs joined them. How many frogs were there then?	The child answers "14" almost immediately and explains, "I know because 6 and 6 is 12 and 2 more is 14."
Fact Recall Eight birds were sitting in a tree. Five flew away. How many are in the tree now?	The child answers "3" immediately and explains, "I know that 8 take away 5 is 3."
Carpenter, T.P., Fennema, E., and Franke, M. L. (1994). Cognitively Guided Instruction: Children's thinking about whole numbers. Madison, WI: Wisconsin Center for Education Research.	

Appendix B

School Board Approval Letter

MEMORANDUM

TO: SHERI MOUSSEAU
FR: GENNY GOLLNICK
RE: REQUEST FROM JUDY HANKES - CGI MATH
DA: OCTOBER 07, 1993

During the 1992-1993 school year, Mrs. Hankes, a math educator from the Wisconsin Center of Educational Research worked with three of our teachers who were implementing the Cognitively Guided Instruction (CGI) teaching approach. This past summer, after being convinced that CGI helps Oneida children understand math, four more Oneida teachers participated in a CGI workshop taught by Mrs. Hankes at the Einstein Academy at Green Bay.

The Oneida CGI teachers agree that this approach builds number sense and understanding and that children with number sense are better problem solvers; however, there is no documentation of the effectiveness of this approach with Oneida children.

Approved Sch Bd Oct 14 1993

This year Mrs. Hankes would like to investigate the influence of CGI in Ana Alicia's Kindergarten classroom. Mrs Hankes is working on her Ph.D. and would use this study for her dissertation. Ana Alicia is willing to participate in such a study. As part of the investigation, Mrs Hankes would also like to interview elders and ask their opinions about the cultural sensitivity of CGI.

I recommend that this be brought to the School Board. I strongly support this request and encourage your support and that of the Board to proceed with this investigation.

Cognitively Guided Instruction is an alternative approach to teaching math that complements many of the culturally unique methods of communication and socialization shared among Native American people.

Cultural Components of this approach are:

1. The math content is problem based and contextualized with the culture and lived experiences of the children. It is not simpl y drill and practice.
2. Children are encouraged to work cooperatively rather than competively.
3. The teacher facilitates so that children construct their own understanding rather than telling children what to do.
4. Enough time is given to allow children to build understanding. Instruction is not time driven but time generous.

In conclusion, Judy Hankes has freely given of her time in staff support of CGI through classroom demonstrations and 1-1 conferencing with teachers. This is what the second grade teacher Elizabeth Timmins thinks of CGI:

> I support Judy Hankes in her implementation of and study of CGI Mathematics at Oneida Tribal School. She was one of my trainers in CGI this past summer. She is very knowledgeable about teaching math in this holistic fashion and she is highly sensitized to the cultural dynamics of our school to which CGI can be a tremendous asset. All I can say about CGI is that I have never enjoyed teaching math so much nor have I ever seen students as enthusiastic about math before. It is exciting, electric learning which respects each child's innate knowledge and acknowledges each child's ability to teach by sharing their thoughts and strategies with others. I am eager to help Judy with her discoveries since she has been so helpful to me in becoming a better teacher. Yaw^ko.

Appendix C

Oneida Culture Documents

1) The Iroquois Creed
2) The Native American Values Seal
3) Oneida Tribal School K–8 Mission Statement

This creed was posted in the hallway of the Oneida School.

The Iroquois Creed

He believed in an all powerful Great Spirit,
in the immortality of the soul, in a life
everlasting and in the fraternity of all life.
With an Iroquois, a thankful heart was prayer.
He did not seek to instruct the Great Creator
what to do on Earth or in the Sky World,
for he had faith in the Creator's wisdom.
The Creator knows what is right and best.
He believed it is natural to be honorable and truthful,
and cowardly to lie.
His promise was absolutely binding.
He hated and despised a liar and
held all falsehood to be a weakness.
He believed in reverence for his parents,
and in their old age, he supported them,
just as he expected his children to support him.
He honored his Father and his Mother and
their Fathers and Mothers before them.

He believed in a forgiving spirit,
preferring atonement to revenge,
in converting enemies into friends.
He believed in peace.
The sentiment of universal brotherhood
was always his policy.
Hospitality was his prime virtue.
No people were more generous.
He did not believe in tyranny,
and he treated his wards with justice,
tolerance, and restraint.
He had no caste system, believing in
democracy, equality, and brotherhood.
And he practiced it.
He coveted not titles,
but believed all men are equal.
He did not covet property either,
and theft among Iroquois was unknown.
He believed in cleanliness of body,
and purity of morals.
Chastity was an established principle with him.
He believed that a truly great man was
one who had done something for his people,
not one who had accumulated more wealth.
He believed the Earth is the mother of all things,
and therefore, no one owned the soil
and no one has more title than another.
His whole civil policy was averse to the concentration
of power in the hands of an individual
but inclined to the opposite principle
of division among equals.
He believed in the equality of women, and
Iroquois women had rights European woman never had.

by Ray Fadden, an Iroquois elder

The researcher recognizes that the wording of this document is sexist. However, the document was selected because it was displayed in the hallway of the Oneida Tribal School, and it succinctly expresses Iroquois Oneida beliefs. Culture informants stressed that the creed should have been written with a female pronoun, since in Iroquois culture the woman is regarded more highly.

It was suggested that Fadden wrote the creed for a non-Indian audience.

Oneida Tribal School K–8 Mission Statement

Culture evolves from universal precepts. Language carries culture norms in an upward spiral which encompasses all community members. Oneida culture concepts flow upward, moving from the general to the specific and back to the general again. The culture concepts seek their own balance as they meet the evolving needs of the people.

The cultural spiral of knowledge brings a higher progression of awareness. All parts of the environment are interdependent. Each part has an integral function that affects the whole. The interweaving of human beings in a social setting and the organisms that thrive in the natural world follow the same natural laws.

Nurturing the individual is the first process. Students will learn pride in their identity. they will learn self-respect which will, in turn, engender respect for others and for everything that exists in the natural world. The personal attributes that will be promoted in the education system include being adaptable to change, having confidence in one's abilities that is refined through self-discipline and willingness to be a self-advocate. Oneida students will leave with a deep understanding of themselves espousing the Oneida value of **REASON**.

Herbs, medicines, and ceremonies are ways of achieving an equilibrium in the body. Students will acquire the capabilities of maintaining balance through the natural environment. The resources provided by the Earth will help create a healthy body. Students will exercise self-control in using the Earth's gifts. Oneidas understand the close relationship between a healthy mind and body. This value is incorporated in the Oneida concept of **PEACE**.

Oneida students will learn they are members of an Oneida community and recognize the responsibilities between the individual and the environment. Responsibilities are acquired through cooperation within the framework of the clan system and through the Oneida language which embodies respect to all living things. The student skills will include active listening, seeing other perspectives, decision making, and arriving at consensus. These responsibilities and skills reflect leadership qualities which are inherent in the Oneida principle of **RIGHTEOUSNESS**. Righteousness is the basic rights practiced between people. By upholding these established rights, students will assure preservation of the environment and survival of the community.

There are many symbols in Oneida culture fostering unity. cultural activities transmit significant teachings and symbolic relationships. Examples include our origins as People of the Great Tree. The arts crafts, songs, dances, and games are both ceremonial and social. These activities promote unity. Their cultural message is derived from the Oneida concept of **POWER** which is a belief system and explains our existence here as human beings. The concept of power, when enforced, are the norms, rules, and customs of society. These laws and customs are based on the authority derived from government and religion.

Oneidas have a unique cultural world. To empower our students as they participate in Western culture, it is important they be given the opportunity to discover and explore their cultural identity first. Students will leave enriched with a positive, coherent sense of self.

It is understood that the educational process for ethnic groups has been and can be destructive or constructive to growth and development. With this in mind,the school will provide opportunities for students to know what is their own in contrast to what belongs to others. Mult-ethnic education leads to higher level thinking skills and appreciation for others. Oneida students will be culturally "literate" in the best sense of the word.

Appendix D

Interview Example

Interview #4

Date: 4-14-94
Kindergarten Teacher
Interviewer: Judith Hankes
Location: Oneida Tribal School, Oneida, Wisconsin

The interview was held in the teacher's classroom while students were at the library. Immediately before the interview, the teacher reread the principles of Native American Pedagogy, and I explained that the purpose of the interview was to focus on whether or not she felt that CGI corresponded with these principles and with Oneida cultural values specifically.

I: How do these (referring to the principles of Native American pedagogy) fit with the Oneida culture, principles of the Oneida culture?

T: I think they are parallel.

I: What I'm really wondering is how does CGI fit in a Native American classroom? Culturally? That's what I would like you to think about. How does it fit culturally?

T: Well, I think it fits culturally just for the fact that with CGI I think you can , well, it's more age appropriate. In the culture, they used to teach when children were ready, and I think that parallels. If that makes any sense.

I: Ya, anything else that you think parallels?

T: The hands on and the visual and the situation where the teacher is guiding them not always telling them, where the teacher is letting them find their own answers, letting them draw conclusions for themselves. Also, I think there's more cooperation, there's more of a group effort. Everybody is encouraged to work together. It's not like they are trying to decide who's the best or who's not the best. It's where they are that's important and what they can contribute to the group.

I: That's the culture?

T: Right.

I: And you see that in CGI?

T: Right, mhm, very much so.

I: Thinking about the way you taught math before CGI, what would you say is the biggest difference between then and now?

T: I guess the biggest difference is I have a better understanding of math and how kids develop, go through stages to get to where they understand, and I know when I used to teach math, the kids just couldn't get it. Now I realize that there are different stages, different developmental stages in problem solving, in how they understand. Now I know it's not the fault of the child. It's just that they are not at that level.

I: So this was new information that you didn't have before?

T: Right, right.

I: Anything else?

T: It's more time generous. I'm not as structured as I used to be when we were in the workbooks. You know, we would have a half an hour for math, and we had to get it all done in that half hour. I also think that with CGI you can integrate it into everything that you do, science or language.

I: Besides knowing the developmental levels, is there anything else that CGI has given you?

T: It just empowers me because I see the kids being successful and them having more confidence.

I: What types of things are you doing that you see this?

T: A lot more visual things like graphing, voting on things and graphing then comparing with the graph. Literature, integrating math into stories that I read aloud and then ask math questions from, and then, integrating the culture more, asking math questions from culture stories.

I: Besides understanding the developmental levels of children's

thinking, was there any other knowledge that allowed you to take

literature and turn it into a math lesson?

T: I don't know what you mean?

I: Before CGI were you able to take a story and develop math problems from it? Did you do that type of thing?

T: Well, I did some story problems, but now, knowing the different problem types, I can interchange different problem types to fit the story. Before I never really did that. I didn't do a lot of story problems.

I: How has the knowledge of CGI helped you instruct, helped you choose problems?

T: I just want to say it gives me the liberty to do it. Does that make sense?

I: The knowledge of the problem types gives you the liberty?

T: The knowledge of the problem types and the way the kids go about solving them, you know, their strategies. Before I didn't know how to do that. I really didn't understand the developmental thinking of children as far as math is concerned. I didn't even understand the math. I just followed the workbook manual and had the kids do what they were supposed to do in the workbook to cover that year, and I always wondered why kids were struggling.

I: Now, my perception of you as a teacher, I assume that before CGI you were a very child-centered teacher.

T: Mhm.

I: And a lot of the things like listening to children, letting children work in teams, a lot of hands-ons activities, things like that were things you did before CGI.

T: Mhm.

I: So, has anything changed about you besides the fact that you're giving story problems and you're listening to children to try to figure out where they are developmentally. Has anything else about your instruction changed?

T: Not a lot. CGI fits in the way I, my teaching style.

I: Would you say, if there was a tribal school where all the teachers shared Native American values, would CGI fit into a Native American style of teaching?

T: Ya, it would depend on the teacher, how in balance that person was with the culture.

I: If you were a culturally balanced Oneida teacher, CGI would fit with the style?

T: Ya.

I: Genny (the Oneida Tribal School curriculum coordinator) and I were talking about this, and I was trying to fit CGI culturally, and Genny was talking about how a good storyteller knows the story and also knows the audience and can adjust the story to the audience. Would you say that CGI gives you the knowledge of math and children's levels of understanding in that same way? Would you say that before CGI you really didn't know the story of math?

T: I never grew up with a real confidence in math so I guess a big thing that changed for me was that now I feel more confident.

I: If you were asked to speak with the administrator of a tribal school, what would you tell that person about CGI?

T: I guess I would tell my personal experiences and how I've seen the changes in the kids that I've worked with, about their success, about them being confident. I think a lot of Indian children don't feel good about school and that's because they haven't had that success.

I: What does that confidence look like? When you know a child is confident about what they are doing with their math, what does that look like?

T: They are happy to engage in math problems. They are happy that, it's not like a pressure that they have to have the right answer or get the page done. They're excited about what they are doing. Kids are working, solving problems because they want to, you know.

I: Ya, I know what you mean. Well, I've asked all the questions I wanted to ask. Anything else that you would like to say about anything?

T: I think that as a Native American person, I think a lot of Native American people are like this, math wasn't something I liked in school, but it's important in life. It's getting more important. Indian kids are going to have to know math if they are going to get through high school and get jobs. If I can help my kids feel good about math, if I can empower them so when they leave my room they take that feeling with them, then that's what I want.

I: And you think CGI helps them do that?

T: I think so.

Appendix E

Culture Analysis

1) Oneida Values
2) Oneida Pedagogy
3) Oneida View of the Child

Culture Value #1—Belief in the Creator Spirit

Curriculum Coordinator

The Creator gave away of himself to make things, to make the universe, to make the rocks, the plants, the stars, and to make all this [gestures to the window and outside]. To us they are like non-entities, they are not people. That was a give-away, and to make that into creation, the Creator had to put essence of himself into all of that, otherwise they wouldn't have existed. The way our creation story explains it is that the first things that were created were thoughts. Those thoughts then became the actual thing, and becoming was the result of some vibration. The Chippewa creation story explains this well. The Sioux creation story does too. I like the Oneida story, but I think those two tribes explain it better. The Creator shared his thoughts and in that sharing created. That's the universal law that existed everywhere (1/3 12-2-93, 19–36).

They looked at a white person coming in as another human being created by the Creator, and when that one human being treats another human being a certain way, with difference, when we know we came from the same source, then it's like that person is not respecting the other's humanity (1/3 12-2-93, 316–20).

The American Indian belief system is that human life came like a spark, a spark that came into existence at one moment, at one moment of existence. You wouldn't call it a human life. You would call it like sparks of life, but the human spirit was different from the things that were created before because it had an Identity with the Creator (1/3 12-2-93, 43–48).

Student Advocate

I believe that the Indian knows the importance of spirituality . . . he knows that he was born into spirituality, and if he chooses to use it, it just furthers his life. It enhances his life (1/1 11-18-93, 181–85).
If you don't teach a child that they have spirituality and that the goodness of people is important, then you're not teaching about spirituality. It's important to let a child know that he is important to the Creator or to God no matter what he might have done. That type of thing is important (1/1 11-18-93, 188–93).

Kindergarten Teacher

People don't seek wisdom, and people don't seek the Creator for their direction. . That's why I think so many things are out of balance in the world because they are not in tune with who created them or what we're supposed to be doing here on Earth (2/5 10-14-93, 4, 44–47).

The most beautiful thing for me is . . . the Creator made me a special person, made me different (2/5 10-14-93, 5, 23–24). We do the Thanksgiving prayer: we are thankful for the sun, we are thankful for the Earth; we are thankful (2/5 10-14-93, 5, 31–33).

I try to teach them balance, that being Oneida doesn't make them best, it just makes them special to the Creator, and there are other cultures and other people out there who are just as special to the Creator (2/5 10-14-93, 7, 38–41).

I feel the gifts I have aren't mine. They are the Creator's, and what I do or what I give to others is not for my glory or to glorify myself. It's to glorify the Creator and to help others along the way (3/5 11-3-93, 94–97).

Elder #1

Well, whether it's Catholic or Longhouse, we are still praying to one God, just one . . . only one we have. All the churches believe that too (1/1 11-3-93, 273–78).

All Indian people have basically the same culture. Like we're saying here [pointing to creed], who we say prayers to, who we give thanks to, and nature (1/1 11-3-93, 306–10).

Elder #2

When we give thanks to the Creator, we use tobacco to make a smudge (1/2 11-18-93, 615–16).

Culture Theme #2: The Importance of Harmony

Curriculum Coordinator

The Creator in his wisdom made polarities so that there would be constant movement, so that there would be constant interchange, and this is what I described as give away. When we talk about male and female and other philosophies like the Oriental ying and yang, but in our teachings we would describe it by explaining that the morning star represents that minute balance between day and night . . . We see in the Earth this duality, this constant change, this constant tension always occurring. As long as they are both respected, both allowed to exist, life goes on . . . what this leads us to is a philosophy of balance and harmony. It isn't that we are trying to attain a middle ground that points where night transforms to day or day to night. We are not trying to catch that very short moment, but we understand that there is balance . . . So that philosophy leads into the study of science, into the study of balance (2/3 12-9-93, 34–60).

Student Advocate

I love harmony. I'm not good at seeking control. I think most Indians want harmony, seek harmony (1/1 11-18-93, 338–39).

Kindergarten Teacher

[The values that I would say are unique to Oneida people are] teaching respect, teaching the children to get along with others, to be in balance with nature, to be in balance with themselves spiritually and mentally and academically and socially (2/5 10-14-93, 1, 34–37).

We were always helpful to everyone, and everybody, I feel, was in harmony back then because decisions were made together, and they were always equal with everything on Earth, and I try to carry that over in my class (2/5 10-14-93, 5, 28–31).

That would be so wonderful, to be at peace. I try to teach the kids about peace, and I try to teach the kids about not only being Oneida, what's good about being Oneida, but I also try to teach them balance, that being Oneida doesn't make them the best, it just makes them special to the Creator, and there are other cultures and other people out there who are just as special to the Creator (2/5 10-14-93, 7, 35–40).

I'm in balance most of the time, and when I'm out of balance, I try to seek the Creator's advice (2/5 10-14-93, 7, 54–56).

Native Americans [believe] in using the medicine wheel it's just being in balance with your spirit—your mental, your physical, your social, and your spiritual. They divide it into four and call it a wheel, and if one of those things is out of sync, then you're not the best that you can be. When all of those things are in harmony, then you are at your best (3/5 11-3-93, 7–11).

I think Oneidas seek harmony rather than seeking control, and I think they look out for the community more than the individual (3/5, 11-3-93, lines 192–94).

I think the people who were our leaders weren't like dictators telling us what to do. They showed us a good way to live with harmony, and they took the time to teach until it was understood (3/5 11-3-93, 272–75).

Elder #2

Every time I do the opening [a recitation given at every social gathering], I mention the Great Tree of Peace. That is very important to us (1/2 11-17-93, 599–601).

Culture Value #3: The Importance of Generosity

Curriculum Coordinator

If you go into an Indian's home and wonder why they are so quiet and non-communicative, it's because they are givers not takers, and they are waiting. They are waiting to hear what you want, what you need, what your request is going to be (1/3 12-2-93, 295–99).

Part of the law of creation was that the Creator was able to give of himself, share of himself, his basic energy, his basic identity, whatever that thing is that the Creator is, and put it into something else. That became the law because that set into play something that continues today that has expanded into many different directions and in many different ways. So, this give-away continues. Otherwise, life stops, ends. So we have ceremonies that promote giving. Because we are human we have to practice those ceremonies to keep the concept, the original teaching, alive. When you have an honor song, an honor dance, that's a give-away. When you offer people food when they walk in the door, that's a give-away. When the Longhouse is set up in moieties and One side does one thing and the other side does something else that's a give-away; there's a sharing cooperation. When we give prayers, we recognize that everything we consume is not ours. We thank that plant or animal for giving itself to us (1, 112–30).

Student Advocate

We are never going to be rich because we don't know how to, you know, how to hoard it. When somebody needs something and we have it, we'll help. So there goes whatever you've tried to save for a while. You want to try to accumulate wealth, but then something happens in the family and you say, "Let them have it. We'll make some more another day." That's pretty much how we've run our lives. That's the way I am, but I really can't say me because I'm really not me. I am a part of a whole family (1/1 11-18-93, 275–84).

It's an honor to do something for somebody else. That's what I kind of grew up under (1/1 11-18-93, 365–66).

Kindergarten Teacher

We're investing more in things than in people, but the original Iroquois Creed would have been that you invest in people, and you seek the best direction and be mindful of everyone's well being so everyone is healthy along the path (2/5 10-14-93, 4, 51–54).

People's own ambition or people seeking to get ahead or power have broken the harmony. Those things really have strong holds on people's lives, and I guess I feel it doesn't help the whole body (2/5 10-14-93, 4, 58, 62; 5, 1).

All the Indian people I know, like my family, they always put you before themselves . . . when I think of my great aunts or my grandmother [they] always wanted to meet your needs first. They always

wanted to invite you in and feed you and clothe you. If you liked something, they would give it to you (2/5 10-14-93, 5, 48–55).
I feel the gifts I have aren't mine. They are the Creator's, and what I do or what I give to others is not for my glory or to glorify myself. It's to glorify the Creator and to help others along the way (3/5 11-3-93, 94–107).

Elder #2

"[The Oneida] were never [greedy]. Even if you go back to the evolutionary war. The Iroquois fed the United States army. They didn't say, you owe me so much money." [It was a] gift (int. 1 of 2, 11-17-93, lines 557–59).

They are not greedy. Right here in Oneida we have got people who are going for wealth, but a true Oneida doesn't look for wealth. You look to help the next people (1/2 11-17-93, 540–42).

Culture Value #4: Importance of Cooperation

Curriculum Coordinator

I think sharing was a concept that began in the beginning, but there are things that came after it to help maintain the concept. I would say cooperation is that. There were like guidelines and rules of behavior and rituals set up and community procedures set up that were cooperative and that helped ensure that sharing kept going on from the past to the present and to the future. So they are related that way (1/3 12-2-93, 8–94).

Student Advocate

I don't want all that goes with leadership. I don't want you to think that I am something better than you. You can lead just as easily as I can (1/1 11-18-93, 266–68).

I would rather everybody shared in whatever achievement there is . . . I don't like to call attention to myself by doing something or having somebody recognize me (1/1 11-18-93, 352–55).

I am part of a whole family. I have never made decisions by myself. We've always had family meetings. When the kids were home, we called a meeting together, and they would share their ideas (1/1 11-18-93, 284–86).

Kindergarten Teacher

I think the Oneidas are real strong in having a real democracy. Everybody contributes to the decision making, and that's the value system that I try to do in my classroom—that everyone has a part, that everyone has to contribute to the decisions we make, good or bad. There's also a value that we talk things out and everyone's opinion is shared in a talking circle (2/5 10-14-93, 1, 36–42).

We are all a family, you know, our tribe. What happens with the tribe effects everyone in the tribe (2/5 10-14-93, 2, 19–22).

I just know that Oneida people really value families, and I think all around in every race the family is a real broken thing now. I think the Oneida people try, and it's still real family oriented (2/5 10-14-93, 3, 12–18).

They believed in equality and democracy and brotherhood, and I really think that. And I really think also that we try to believe that all people are equal (2/5 10-14-93, 5, 60–62).

What I know of the traditional ways, everyone had part of the decisions. You know that's why they had clans and discussed things and they all came together, and they didn't leave till they all agreed (2/5 10-14-93, 3, 40–44

We explain to the kids about nature and how we are equal . . . and just explain to them how important everything is. Everything has a purpose (3/5 11-3-93, 27–29).

I feel I am modest. Oneidas don't like to show themselves to be better than others. Like when we started doing this research, I didn't want to be above everybody else (3/5 11-3-93, 88–91).

I think the way that the culture was, there was such a democracy where everyone had a part, everybody had their part, and it was always what was best for the group, that kind of living arrangement (3/5 11-3-93, 116–19).

I think as a culture, as a community, one of the other teachers said this too, it's not just the parents who raise the child, it's the community. I think that that is true on a reservation, the children are influenced by the community (3/5 11-3-93, 189–91).

Elder #1

This is our belief [pointing to the creed]. Years ago there were families here. They were all together . . . and in the community everyone helped each other (1/1 11-3-93, 353–54).

Our idea is to cooperate, work together. Of course, half the time we don't do it, but that's what we try (1/1 11-3-93, 392–93).

Elder #2

In the old way there was more sharing of leadership, but not now. I hate to say that, but we don't know what's going on . . . it shouldn't be that way (2/3 12-2-93, 93–96).

[In the old way] the group decided until there was a tie or something, and then the chief decided. The chief had nothing to say until there was a tie (1/2 11-17-93, 125–27).

Pedagogical Principle #1: Cooperation Rather than Competition

Curriculum Coordinator

I think sharing was a concept that began in the beginning, but there are things that came after it to help maintain the concept. I would say cooperation is that. There were guidelines and rules of behavior and rituals set up and community procedures set up that were cooperative and that helped ensure that sharing kept going on from the past, to the present, and to the future (1/3 12-2-93, 131–38).

Student Advocate

[As far as individual or group achievement] I would rather everybody shared in whatever achievement there is than just myself. I don't like to call attention to myself by doing something or having somebody recognize me (1/1 11-18-93, lines 352–55).

[With grades] somebody has to feel bad . . . at the public school I feel very sorry for our students. I believe that some of them are trying their best and don't come anywhere near someone who is really achieving well. Even if they are good, they don't feel that they are because these others, on their report cards, have come up real high and they haven't. If one student was always getting As and everybody always commented about her As and I couldn't come up with anything more than a C or a D, then I would say, "Why am I trying?" (1/1 11-18-93, 471–82).

Kindergarten Teacher

I think the Oneidas are real strong in democracy. Everyone contributes to the decision making, and that's the value system that I try to do in my classroom—that everyone has a part, that everyone has to contribute to the decisions we make, good or bad. There's also a value that we talk things out, and everyone's opinion is shared in a talking circle (2/5 10-14-93, 1, 38–42).

We were always helpful to everyone, and everybody, I feel, was in harmony back then because decisions were made together, and they were always equal with everything on Earth, and I try to carry that over with my class (2/5 10-14-93, 5, 28–32).

I try to incorporate other kids to help, cooperative learning, so that we're all learning together, that we all want to feel good about learning (2/5 10-14-93, 8, 4–17).

I think a teacher has to meet the individual needs. If they are a little bit further, then they have to be challenged, but my kids who are brighter help the other kids. I do that as cooperative learning, and we talk a lot about how some people are good at this, and others are better at something else, and that they are best at one thing. We just have to find it [what they are best at]. I always plan my lessons so that every level will have success and they'll feel good about sharing that. And we talk a lot about not embarrassing another person (3/5 11-3-93, 59–68).

Elder #1

That is our idea to cooperate, work together . . . that's what we try (1/1 11-3-93, 392–93).

Pedagogical Principle #2: Indirect Rather Than Direct Instruction

Curriculum Coordinator

Indian people, when they teach, they teach from where the person they are talking to is coming from and bring them along one step at a time. They don't say, "Hey, we want you to jump a mile here," because they know they will lose them. So, the Indian teacher will only lead the audience one step. [The Native American listens to a person to find out where they are.] (1/3 12-2-93, 259–68).

The authority figure, that's where the cross-cultural conflict enters. The authority figure comes in, and ya, ya, they (the students) evaluate the authority figure. I think they will instantly size that person up as having bad manners, being ill-mannered . . . they will see that that person must be so wrapped up in himself (1/3 12-2-93, 310–14).

What I see happening is that when a new teacher comes in, if that young child was taught in the home how to treat other folks, then there's regard for humanity. There's regard given to the essence of who we are, and if that's there, and a child sees that lived in front of them—they see their parent's behavior, their old brother's and sister's behavior, how guests are treated; well, when they are in the classroom, they expect to be treated the same way that they are at home . . . I think in the classroom that the students are kind of appalled when a non-native teacher comes in and acts like an authoritarian, acts like they know everything. Here's this young child of five, seven, or nine thinking this way, and they know in their own families that this would not be culturally accepted or approved . . . Social status goes to the people who can share and care the most, and if a teacher tries to impress by throwing out this vast body of knowledge, that runs counter to what is good or what is great about living. So they look at a non-native teacher behaving that way as being kind of like a person who is almost sick. You know, they have to get themselves together (1/3 12-2-93, 337–61).

Student Advocate

I think they [referring to the elders and the old way] just laid it on them and let them figure it out, and then if they weren't correct, they would ask, "Did you figure that in?" That's how I think they taught (1/1 1-18-93, lines 436–39).

With my mother, way back, even in adding would say, "Try it. Show me that you can do it." Then after proving that I could do it or that I couldn't, then she would tell me which way I should go. But I remember she wanted me to try it (1/1 11-18-93, 442–46).

I hate to have somebody talk to me, and some teachers talk in monotone voices so after a while your mind is gone. It's outside someplace. You're doing something else. It's better to have then do it and then talk about it (1/1 11-18-93, 462–66).

I would give the problem and they would do what they could do with it, go back over and see what has been done and see why they did it this way and if it can be done a different way, then talk about that, but just let them do it on their own first. (1/1 11-18-93, 526–28).

Kindergarten Teacher

I don't know everything. We are a body of learners together, and they [the students] can teach me things, and I can teach them things. They don't have to address me, they are respectful to me, but they don't have to address me as though I am better or know more (2/5 10-14-93, 2, 38–42).

I want them to feel they are equal to me, that they can ask me anything, that they can be participators in their learning, that they can be involved in what's going on in our classroom (2/5 10-14-93, 2, 47–49).

[You find out their strengths by] getting to know what they want to learn about, incorporating what they want to learn about, you know, facilitating what needs to be learned. In a way, that's a real good balance, and with that the kids are happy with their learning balance (2/5 10-14-93, 3, 24–28).

I never try and single out a kid and say, "Oh you're the worst or your the best academically I try and meet them at their level where they can find success" (2/3 10-14-93, 8, 13–15).

Elder #1

The teacher is filling in for them, and so she's their crutch. They look at her and their problem is solved. They don't have to think . . . The teacher shouldn't [tell them how to do things] (1/1 11-3-93, 561–63).

I don't feel comfortable like that [standing at the front of the room teaching](1/1 11-3-93, 450–51).

You sit with them [she spreads her hands in a circle]. You sit with them (1/1 11-3-93, 458–59).

Elder #2

I talk to them just like it is outside, right there [gesturing out the window], not in school, I talk to them (1/2 11-17-93, 84–85).

Pedagogical Principle #3: Hands-on problem solving

Curriculum Coordinator

Observational lessons are probably the most basic American Indian scientific teaching method (2/3 12-9-93, 99–102).

To a group of students we tell the story and then ask, "What is this story describing? What is it all about? What do you understand about this story?, and if they don't make the connection, I give a hands-on activity that helps them make the connection. An example is a real neat Blackfoot story about the rolling stone, and the stone having thoughts about what was given to it and taken from it. At the beginning of the lesson everyone is given a stone . . . at the end we mix up all of the stones and each person has to find the original stone . . . but the reason it was able to happen is because they had held a stone" (2/3 12-9-93, 114–36).

Student Advocate

I think they just laid it on them, let them figure it out, then if they weren't correct, they would ask, "Did you figure this in? Did you figure that in? That's how I think they taught" (1/1 11-18-93, 436-439).

I know a lot of children in schools who didn't learn if the teacher tried to teach outwardly. This way [gesturing away from herself]. But if they got something their students could work with their hands on, they could do it. I think I'm still that way. I hate to have somebody talk to me, and some teachers talk in monotone voices so after a while your mind is gone. It's outside someplace. You're doing something else. It's better to have them do it and then talk about it (1/1 11-18-93, 458–66).

[If I was teaching Oneida children], they would get the problem, and they would do what they could do with it. [I would] just let them do it on their own first (1/1 11-18-93, 525–28).

Kindergarten Teacher

I think hands-on is easier, instructing them in a way that they can do it themselves. I think that's kind of traditionally how they did things, real oral kind of passing it down from generation to generation. It's a more hands-on approach (2/5 10-14-93, 9, 23–26).

I think that with the old way, when a problem would arise, it was looked at as something to learn from (3/5 11-3-93, 255–56).

Elder #1

[I teach through] pictures that they would do themselves, how they would like it to be. Then from there we work together (1/1 11-2-93, 410–12).

You learn by doing . . . I think [that was] the way (1/1 11-2-93, 464–67).

Elder #2

I think they've got to act it through. If you simply have them do work, work, well, then the next day, they don't know what the word was, but make them act it, all of them. Like here [reaches to his desk for a list of vocabulary words]. These are all pronouns. I have them act it or draw it. They got to go through all that (2/2 12-2-93, 129-34).

Pedagogical Principle #4: Culturally Situation Problem Solving

Curriculum Coordinator

Indian people are observers first. The first teaching method is to observe. As students collect data and learn about the environment, they are learning about this major philosophy [the philosophy of harmony and balance] through observation. They see in the rocks, the plants, the animals, the trees, the air, all of the natural forces around them exemplify this [harmony and balance]. In fact, all of the stories contain these observations. So if a teacher collected the traditional stories, they would start to understand how Indian folks observed all of this, how the contradictions of life and nature really fit together and is interconnected (2/3 12-9-93, 61–71).

Kindergarten Teacher

Learning from daily experiences, that you're taking from their lives something that's valid and turning that into something that helps them learn. I try to incorporate the culture and what we are working on and what's important to them. Like this year, I have a little boy in the classroom with leukemia. So we are trying to learn about cancer (3/5 11-3-93, 244–50).

Elder #1

I would teach them the language at my house. Plus, afterwards we would eat, and then they would know how to give thanks and how to say words at the table (1/1 11-2-93, 429–32).

See, we do more storytelling. Wherever I've gone to workshops among different tribes, you know, that's what they always tell us, "Start with storytelling," and I believe that because that's how I learned . . . we go to workshops where, for some reason, we all have the same culture, no matter what different tribes we are. Basically, they all say storytelling, and that's not a hard way (1/1 11-2-93, 481–87).

[You learn from storytelling because] that's what you grew up knowing (1/1 11-2-93, 489).

Elder #2

Now this morning, the pre-kindergarten, I had this conversation with them about running. I said, "You tell me here that this boy is a runner." Cuz this boy was telling her that he was a runner, and she was telling me that. So I thought this would be a good time to have them listen. I had her tell me in the language. They caught on. Then on the other side, I'm trying to get the same thing. I said, "You saw what's going on. You do the same thing. You tell that girl." I'm always trying to get the Oneida words out there. You see, 'boy running' is an Oneida word, but 'girl runner' is a different word, but they have the stem in there that's the same. We keep going like that (2, 103–13). I talk to them just like it is outside, right there, not in school. I talk to them (2/2 12-2-93, 84–85).

Pedagogical Principle #5: Time Generous Rather Than Time-Driven

Student Advocate

[If I could teach the way I wanted] they would get the problem, and they would do what they could do with it, and then after that's done, go back over and see what they have done and see why they did it this way and if it can be done a different way, then talk about that, but then just let them do it on their own first, and give them all the time they need to do it (1/1 12-18-93, 524–30).

Kindergarten Teacher

I think Indian people have their own time. I think that the learning process always continues. It is not like on a time thing, like you're supposed to learn this at, you should know it by now, or like at one o'clock you should know everything, or whatever the time is, that you should have all the answers or tests and stuff like that. I think that when you learn, you're continually learning and adding to your base, and that's, I think, how Native Americans taught each other a long time ago, but because we live in such a time-constrained world, I guess we carry that over too. But I think Indian people are not very punctual. I know we never were (2/5 10-14-93, 10, 1-6).

I don't think you learn that way [time rushed]. Culturally they would just keep at something until little by little you learned it. And now, I think in school systems you learn this by three o'clock because we are going onto the next page. Lots of times the kids don't get it. And I think culturally, when they did it orally, they went on for days and months with the same things until everyone got it. It was really laid back. They took the time to meet all their other needs too (3/5 11-3-93, 175–80).

I think you need to give time to kids, generous time to kids to feel good about themselves and then to learn. We don't do that. We rush them, and then they feel failure (3/5 11-3-93, 300–02).

I think that the old way, when a problem would arise, it was viewed as something to learn from. They weren't on a timeline, so they would take the time to teach that (3/5 11-3-93, 255–57).

They took the time to teach until it was understood. I think that was true for the culture and I want that for my kids. I don't want to be like hollering or giving someone the feeling that they are dumb because they don't get it when I think they should. I want them to be able to get it when they are able to understand and use it for themselves (3/5 11-3-93, 275–83).

Oneida View of the Child

Curriculum Coordinator

I really think that they believe that a child is born as a unique person and that they are already wise, maybe wiser than adults and the children lose some of that wisdom as they grow and become adults. The child is definitely not considered a blank slate. As a matter of fact, a child is considered a gift or a prize to a family, that this child is given as a gift, and the family has to protect, treasure, nurture, and enjoy this person, this other human being, this child for a little while, and then they have to move on. You see, we also have this belief in missions, that everyone has an individual mission. It may be something as simple as being a mom or being a good aunt to one or two people or it could be a major mission. They are born with that mission, a good mission. They might not quite know what that is. So, you give the little children room and space and respect because they, like yourself, have something to do in this life (1/3 12-2-93, 393–410).

Kindergarten Teacher

I think Oneida people value their children and their elders. They want to do the best for them. I think about this when I'm teaching the kids (2/5 10-14-93, 1, 43–45).

One of the things that's passed along through culture is the belief that what we do today is going to benefit the next seven generations, and that is the Great Law. So we have to be mindful of how we are treating the kids. What we do and how we effect them now is going to carry on for the next seven generations (2/5 10-14-93, 2, 4–8).

We are a body of learners together, and they [the students] and I can teach them things. They don't have to address me, they are respectful to me, but they don't have to address me as though I'm better or know more (2/5 10-14-93, 2, 39–42).

I want them to feel that they are equal to me, that they can be participators in their learning, that they can be involved with what's going on in our classroom (2/5 10-14-93, 2, 47–49).

I think every creation is special and God gives you special gifts, and every child has strengths, and I think as teachers, you need to bring out those strengths and have that child feel confident abut something that they can do the very best (2/5 10-14-93, 3, 17–20).

Elder #1

They know more than you think they do (1/1 11-3-93, 426).

Elder #2

She [his grandmother] always had a lot of respect for a child, a lot of respect for a child. We were instructed never abuse, like, well, just like it is today, they'll remember it. There's a day coming that they will be taking our place, and they'll know how to carry on our ancestry, the beliefs and stuff like that (2/2 12-2-93, 28–33).

[My grandfather] said to show respect because he used to say that there was a day coming that they [the children] would be taking our place (2/2 12-2-93, 71–73).

Appendix F

Participating Teacher's Comments Before CGI

Responses to a Brief Questionaire Summer 1992

The teacher was asked to respond to the following questions before participating in the CGI Level I workshop. She had no knowledge of CGI when when these responses were made.

1. What is your role as a teacher during a math lesson?
2. What is the role of the student?
3. What is your philosophy about teaching math?

Responses:

My role is to create a learning environment that introduces math in creative and culturally relevant ways using the seasons, moons, legends. Also providing hands-on ways to introduce basic K concepts: numbers, addition, subtraction, time pattern, size, etc.

The student's role is to to be free and see math as useful and fun and an everyday learning tool—not a chore or drill.

My math philosophy is to use their culture and daily experiences to introduce and make math fun and to help children feel success in the process.

Appendix G

Topical Interview Analysis

Topic 1: The Teacher's Beliefs about the Compatibility of CGI with Oneida/Native American Culture

I guess why I want to do CGI math or why I'm involved in this research is because I value Indian children. I want them to be as successful as they can be, and I know this way is right for them. A lot of times they have to overcome such great obstacles just to be who they are and know who they are. So, if by doing this, I can help any other Indian child, it doesn't have to be Oneida, be better or find what they're best at, that's why I'm doing it (2, 34–41).

I think it fits culturally just for the fact that with CGI it's more age appropriate. In the culture they used to teach when children were ready, and I think that parallels. . . . The hands-on and the visual and the situation where the teacher is guiding them, not telling them, where the teacher is letting them find their own answers, letting them draw conclusions for themselves. Also, I think there's more cooperation, more of a group effort. Everybody is encouraged to work together. It's not like they are trying to decide who is the best or who is not the best. It's where they are that's important and what they can contribute to the group. That's culture, and I see that in CGI (4, 7–27).

CGI would fit into a Native American style of teaching depending how in balance that person was with the culture. Ya, it would fit if you were a culturally balanced teacher (4, 94–101).

(If I was going to tell a tribal school administrator about CGI) I would tell my personal experience and how I've seen the changes in the kids I have worked with, about their success, about them feeling confident. I think a lot of Indian children don't feel good about school, and that's because they haven't had that success (4, 115–19).

I think that as a Native American person, I think a lot of Native American people are like this, math wasn't something I like in school, but it's important in life. It's getting more important. Indian kids are going to have to know math if they are going to get through high school and get jobs. If I can help my kids feel good about math, if I can empower them so when they leave my room they take that feeling with them, then that's what I want. (CGI helps do that.) I think so (4, 131–40).

Topic #2: The Teacher's Beliefs about how CGI Influenced Her Students

I see the kids, how they're having fun (1, 53).

That kind of stuff (counting by tens) is more age appropriate, and they like it, and they're using their own process. There's no right or wrong way (1, 82–84).

They're talking with a lot more . . . they always want to ask what's more now. Anything that we do . . . they are asking math questions (1, 221–27).

I guess I feel I have underestimated them all this time, that, because of all the developmental stuff that I've read, that they can only do this at this age, but they can do far more. They are very bright. I mean, they process it . . . I look at them differently now (1, 344–50).

Usually we don't take the time to see how far they can count (at beginning of kindergarten). We just think they can count to 20, and a lot of them went to 50 (1, 315–17).

(What does CGI mean?) I guess for me it means freedom. It gives the kids the freedom to problem solve for themselves in a naturally, age appropriate way, and it's challenging, and it's fun . . . they talk about that you should be doing things cognitively, and I see that it's working in that they don't feel bad about math. They like it (1, 570–75).

The kids are noticing things more because they are talking about math so much . . . I know that they are looking at their world in a different way (1, 580–87).

Why I really like CGI math is because everybody can find success at their level, everybody can be involved. You have the kids who are counting everything and the kids who are counting by tens, but everybody gets the answer, and everybody feels successful (2, 30–34).

(If asked to tell a tribal school administrator about CGI) I would tell my personal experiences and how I've seen the changes in the kids that I have worked with, about their success, about their confidence. . . . They are happy to engage in math problems. It's not like there's pressure that they have to have the right answer or get the page done. They're excited about what they are doing. Kids are working, solving problems because they want to (4, 115–27).

If I can help my kids feel good about math, if I can empower them so when they leave my room they take that feeling with them, then that's what I want. (CGI helps them do that?) I think so (4, 136–40).

Topic #3: How CGI Influenced the Teacher's Instruction

[We're doing] more hands-on, more counting things, comparing things. Like, this week we did a unit on fall. So we collected all the acorns we could find and we counted. We counted! Usually we would have stopped at twenty, but now we counted to 459. . . . We counted it first in tens [into groups of ten by one] and then we counted it [the groups] by ten. We made groups of tens all around the room, and then we counted them. So, the kids are starting to know numbers beyond 25, that's what they're supposed to know in kindergarten, but they like to go on (1, 60–79).

(Last year) we would still be in the workbook just identifying numbers. I really haven't emphasized on the number line identifying numbers . . . but they see the numbers. I usually write them down (from the story problems), and they get it (1, 189–96).
from them (1, 330–32).

This (CGI) just seems more natural. I make lessons from what intrigues them (1, 261–67).

It seems that I'm always doing math (laugh). Before, I always had a set time. I took about 35 minutes to present, and then we did our little worksheets, but now we just do a lot more, when we do our exploring or whatever, our story problems, it's more intertwined in everything that we do. Sometimes we will pick it up at the end of the day, or if there's a problem that they want to solve, we'll stop and figure it out. So, I feel like we're doing more math. Like today we made applesauce and we were talking about how many cups, and how many pieces you get if you cut an apple in half and then in half again, stuff like that. Math's just more into everything (1, 289–302).

(Last year's math curriculum) I didn't like it at all. The kids were really frustrated. I didn't understand some of the stuff they had to do . . . the worksheets, the way they were laid out, and the instructions were hard for them. It's not that they were anymore difficult. I t was where they had to circle the right answer all of the time, and they didn't have to think about math (1, 259–77).

I do story problems a lot, and usually I'll try to incorporate them into my reading series . . . I'll take the story problems from them (1, 330–32).

(This approach) gives them the freedom to think, to problem solve for themselves and come up with answers that don't have to be right or wrong . . . I tell them that it doesn't matter if it's right or wrong, I'm more concerned with what you think and how you did it, and you're friends are going to check your work, and I don't know what's the right answer. We're on equal ground now because they know that I don't have all the answers all the time, and I have to figure it out myself (1, 412–21).

I've incorporated my own stuff. I make a lot of my own ideas, and I'm not relying on a workbook (1, 519–21).

I guess the biggest difference is I have a better understanding of math and how kids develop, go through stages to get where they understand. I know when I used to teach math, the kids just couldn't get it. Now I realize that there are different stages, different developmental stages in problem solving, in how they understand. Now I know it's not the fault of the child. It's just that they are not at that level (4, 31–38).

It's more time generous. I'm not as structured as I used to be when we were in the workbooks. You know, we would have a half an hour for math, and we had to get it all done in that half hour. I also thing with CGI you can integrate it into everything that you do, science or language (4, 42–46).

Now I'm doing a lot more visual things like graphing, voting on things, then graphing and asking questions about the graph, having them compare. And now I use literature, integrate math into stories that I read aloud and then ask math questions from, and I integrate the culture more, ask math questions from culture stories (4, 52–56).

(Before CGI) I did some story problems, but now, knowing the different problem types, I can interchange different problems to fit the story. Before I never really did that. I didn't do a lot of story problems. CGI gives me the liberty to do it (choose story problems) (4, 64–67, 73–80).

Topic 4: Teacher's Personal Feelings about Mathematics before and after The CGI Workshop and Implementation Experience

Personally, I never really liked math, but I'm learning to be more appreciative of it since I've been using CGI. Now it's a lot more fun, and I'm finding more ways to incorporate it in my classroom, and as I see the kids how they're having fun, it makes me want to challenge them more (1, 48–54).

My aide is, I think she's in shock because she just doesn't know where I'm coming from with all this stuff. (Math ideas) are just in my head now. They just come out when I'm thinking about CGI, thinking about the ways of doing it, and they're just naturally little fun things that we're doing, and math is fun for them now (1, 475–85).

I guess it has given me a little boost as far as I feel good about it. If I feel that they feel good, it makes me feel good, and it makes me want to challenge them more, and it gives me confidence to develop my own things (1, 544–50).

(Why I like CGI is) everybody can feel successful. I can remember not being so successful in math. I still have a math phobia. So, it's real uplifting and real nice to see these little kids enjoying math (2, 30–36).

It just empowers me because I see the kids being successful and them having more confidence (4, 49–50).

I understand the problem types, and I'm beginning to understand the way kids go about solving them, their strategies. Before I didn't know how to do that. I really didn't understand the developmental levels of thinking as far as math is concerned. I didn't even understand the math. I just followed the workbook manual and had the kids do what they were supposed to do in the workbook to cover that year, and I always wondered why kids were struggling (4, 73–80).

I never grew up with a real confidence in math, so I guess a big thing that changed for me is that now I feel more confident (4, 110–12).

I think that as a Native American person, I think a lot of Native American people are like this, math wasn't something I liked in school (4, 131–33).

I see the kids how they're having fun. It makes me want to challenge them more. So, in planning things, I have the freedom to do that now. Before, we did the workbooks, and we did them the way that they said (1, 53–56).

Appendix H

Parent Consent Letter

Oneida Tribal School
ONAYOTE? A·KA TSI?
THUWATILIHUNYANITHA

P.O. Box 365
Oneida, Wisconsin 54155-0365
(414) 869-4308 OR 869-4423

March 1994

Dear Parents:

Your child's teacher, Ana Alicia, has been participating in the Cognitively Guided Instruction project at the Oneida Tribal School for the past two years. This is a project that looks at how children think about and solve math story problems. The project also looks at how a young child's understanding of mathematics can be developed through situating instruction in the cultural and lived experiences of the child. The main purpose of the project is to help young children develop a good number sense and mathematical understanding.

A lot of exciting things are happening in Ana's classroom, and I would like to capture some of what is happening on videotape, with photographs, and in student interviews - the interviews will allow me to find out how Ana's students feel about math as well as determine whether Cognitively Guided Instruction helps them develop better math sense. Part of the reason that I am recording these wonderful experiences is so that they can be shared with other Native American schools as well as math educators. However, this data will not be used to single out or evaluate your child in any way; your child will never be specifically identified.

The videotaping and interviewing will be carried out so that regular classroom instruction will not be interrupted. The board members, administrators, and teachers at the Oneida Tribal School have given their support for documenting this project. In addition, we need your permission to videotape and interview your child. Please sign the attached form and return it to Ana Alicia. If you have any questions, please call Ana or me.

Thank you very much.

Sincerely,

Judith Hankes
Phone: (608)263-9477

+ - - - + - + + - + + - + + - -

Please check one:

____YES. I give my permission to videotape, photograph, and interview my child. I understand that this data will be used for instruction and research purposes.

____NO. I do not give permission to videotape, photograph, and interview my child.

____________	____________	____________
(child's name)	(signature of parent or guardian)	(date)

Oneida Nation in Wisconsin

Appendix I

Oneida Kindergarten Solution Strategy Analysis

Analysis of Oneida Kindergarten Solution Strategies

Separate (Result Unknown)

All seventeen children used a valid strategy for the separate (Result Unknown) problem. All seventeen children directly modeled the action in the problem by making a set of 13 counters, removing 6 of them, and counting the remaining counters.

Join (Change Unknown)

Thirteen children used a valid strategy for the Join (Change Unknown) problem. Nine children directly modeled the problem solution by making a set of 7 counters and adding on counters until there was a total of 11. Two children used a strategy that did not directly model the action in the problem. One child made a set of 11 counters and a set of 7 counters and then lined them up one-to-one correspondence. The other child linked 11 counters together, recounted 7 of the counters, and then separated the 4 remaining counters. Two children counted up from 7 to 11.

Compare

Thirteen children used a valid strategy for the Compare problem. All thirteen directly modeled the problem by constructing the two distinct sets described in the problem, lining the two sets up in one-to-one correspondence, and counting the difference.

Multiplication

Sixteen children used a valid strategy for the Multiplication problem. All sixteen children modeled the problem by making three sets with 6 counters in each set and then counting the three sets of 6.

Measurement Division

Thirteen children used a valid strategy for the Measurement Division problem. Eleven of the children first counted out a collection of 15 counters, put them in sets of 3, and counted the number of sets. Two children also made five sets of 3 counters each, but they did not initially count out 15 counters. Instead, they kept track of the total number of counters used as they constructed their sets. When they had counted out a total of 15 counters in groups of three, they counted the number of sets.

Partitive Division

Thirteen children used a valid strategy for the Partitive Division problem. All children directly modeled the problem making four sets with the same number of counters in each set to find the answer. There was two basic variation of this strategy. Three children systematically dealt the 20 counters one by one into four groups. Ten children made four groups of counters and adjusted the numbers in each group until the groups each contained the same number of counters and all of the counters were used up. Five of the ten children started out making four groups of 4 counters each and then added a counter to teach group. The other five children used a variety of trial and error strategies to equalize the groups.

Division with Remainder

Twelve children used an appropriate strategy for the division problem in which they ad to take into account that a whole car was needed to take care of the extra children. The problem is a measurement division problem, and they modeled it as such.

Multistep

Fourteen children used a valid strategy for the multistep problem. All fourteen used counters to model the problem by making three groups of 4 counters and then removing 5 of the counters.

Nonroutine

For the problem in which 19 children had to be divided up 2 or 3 to a seat in a bus, responses were coded as correct if the children identified the number of seats that were occupied by two children and three children or if they identified the number of children who rode two to a seat and the number who rode three to a seat. Ten children used a valid strategy. Six children designated the seven seats with a counter and systematically dealt the 19 counters out into the seven groups. The other four children used trial and error to place the counters in seven groups containing either 2 or 3 counters.

	SRU	JCU	C	M	MD	PD	D/re	M/step	NRTIN
A	X			X		X			
B	X	X	X	X	X	X	X	X	X
C	X	X	X	X	X	X	X	X	X
D	X	X	X	X	X	X	X	X	
E	X	X	X	X	X	X	X	X	X
F	X			X					
G	X	X	X	X	X	X		X	
H	X	X	X	X	X	X	X	X	X
I	X					X			
J	X			X		X		X	
K	X	X	X	X	X		X	X	X
L	X	X	X	X	X		X	X	X
M	X	X	X	X	X	X	X	X	X
N	X	X	X	X	X	X	X	X	X
O	X	X	X	X	X	X	X	X	X
P	X	X	X	X	X	X	X	X	X
Q	X	X	X	X	X	X	X	X	
Total	17	13	13	16	13	13	12	14	10
%	100	76	76	94	76	76	61	82	59

Percentiles of Children Correctly Solving Word Problems in Six CGI Kindergarten Classrooms (N70)

Total	62	56	60	60	51	49	45	47	41
%	89%	80%	71%	86%	73%	70%	64%	67%	59%
Source: Carpenter, 1993									

Performance of 17 Oneida Kindergartners

Name: A (R. C.)
Age: 6 yrs. 3 mo.
Birthdate: 1/30/88
Date: May 19, 1994 (tape C)

Problem #1 SRU Correct: yes	Strategy: direct model—sets out 13 cubes, separates 6 cubes, counts remaining cubes
Problem #2 JCU Correct: no	Strategegby: direct model—sets out 7, set s out 11, becomes confused
Problem #3 C Correct: no	Strategy: direct model—sets out 12 cubes, sets out 7 cubes, keeps naming the number of cubes in each group, solves with help
Problem #4 M Correct: yes	Strategy: direct model—sets out 3 sets of 6, counts sets together
Problem #5 MD Correct: no	Strategy: direct model—sets out 3 sets of 6, counts sets together
Problem #6 PD Correct: yes Miscount	Strategy: direct model—sets out 20 cubes, sets out 4 markers, distributes one at a time, counts and adjusts til 20 distributed counts number in each group
Problem #7 D/re Correct: no	Strategy: not given
Problem #8 Multistep Correct: yes	Strategy: direct model—sets out 3 markers, distributes 4 cubes to each of the 3, separates 5, counts remaining cubes
Problem #9 Nonroutine Correct: no	Strategy: not given

Name: B (T. D.)
Age: 6 hrs.
Birthdate:
Date: May 17, 1994 (tale A1)

Problem #1 SRU Correct: yes	Strategy: direct model—sets out 13 cubes, removes 6, counts remaining cubes
Problem #2 JCU Success: yes	Strategy: direct model—sets out 7 cubes, joins 4 more with fingers to make 11, counts number joined
Problem #3 C Correct: yes	Strategy: direct model—lines up 12 cubes, lines up 7 cubes, matches, counts the difference
Problem #4 M Correct: yes	Strategy: direct model—sets out 3 markers, distributes 6 cubes to each of the 3, counts
Problem #5 MD Correct: yes	Strategy: direct model—sets out 15 cubes, sets out 3 markers, distributes three to each marker, adds 2 more markers, counts groups
Problem #6 PD Correct: yes	Strategy: direct model—sets out 20 cubes sets out 4 markers, distributes 5 cubes ata time to the 4, counts number of cubes in each group
Problem #7 D/re Correct: yes	Strategy: direct model—sets out 19 cubes, sets out 5 markers, distributes 5 cubes to 3 of the markers and one cube to one of the markers, removes the extra marker, counts groups, it's okay if one group has 4
Problem #8 Multistep Correct: yes	Strategy: direct model—sets out 3 cubes, distributes 4 cubes to each of the 3, removes 5, counts remaining cubes
Problem #9 Nonroutine Correct: yes	Strategy: direct model—sets out 19 cubes, distributes 6 sets of 3, splits a group of 3, counts groups of 2 and groups of 3

Name: C (A.D.)
Age: 5 yrs. 9 mo.
Birthdate: 8/4/88
Date: May 12, 1994 (tape A2)

Problem #1 SRU Correct: yes	Strategy: direct model—sets out 13 cubes, removes 6, counts remaining cubes
Problem #2 JCU Correct: yes	Strategy: direct model—sets out 7 cubes, joins 4 more cubes, counts cubes joined
Problem #3 C Correct: yes	Strategy: direct model—sets out 12 cubes, sets out 7 cubes, lines up and matches, counts difference
Problem #4 M Correct: yes	Strategy: direct model—sets out 3 cubes, distributes 6 cubes to each of the 3 cubes, counts
Problem #5 MD Correct: yes	Strategy: direct model—sets out 15 cubes, separates into groups of 3, places next to markers, counts number of groups
Problem #6 PD Correct: yes	Strategy: direct model—sets out 20 cubes sets out 4 cubes, distributes the 20 cubes to the 4 cubes 5 at a time, lucky guess cubes one at a time, counts number in each group
Problem #7 D/re Correct: yes	Strategy: direct model—sets out 4 markers, distributes 5 cubes at a time, counts cubes, removes extra cube, counts groups, it's alright for one group to have 4
Problem #8 Multistep Correct: yes	Strategy: direct model—sets out 3 markers, distributes 4 cubes to each of the 3, counts remaining cubes
Problem #9 Nonroutine Correct: yes	Strategy: direct model—sets out 7 markers, distributes 2 and 3 cubes to marker alternating, counts groups

Name: D (T.E.)
Age: 6 years
Birthdate: 5/23/88
Date: May 17, 1994 (tape B)

Problem #1 SRU Correct: yes	Strategy: direct model—sets out 13, seperates 7, counts remaining cubes
Problem #2 JCU Correct: yes	Strategy: direct model—sets out 7, joins on, counts number joined
Problem #3 C Correct: yes	Strategy: direct model—sets out 12, sets out 7, matches, counts difference
Problem #4 M Correct: yes	Strategy: direct model—sets out 3 markers, distributes 6 cubes to each, counts total
Problem #5 MD Correct: no	Strategy: direct model—sets out 4 markers, distributes three to each marker, adds another marker, distributes remaining 3, counts aloud to keep track of number distributed, counts number of groups
Problem #6 PD Correct: yes	Strategy: direct model—sets out 20, sets out 4 cubes, distributes the 20 cubes randomly and adjust number of cubes, gets confused, solves with help
Problem #7 D/re Correct: yes	Strategy: direct model—distributes by making groups of 5, repeatedly counting until 19 cubes have been distributed, atates that there are 4 groups, it's okay if one group has 4 cubes
Problem #8 Multistep Correct: yes	Strategy: direct model—sets out 3 markers, distributes 4 to each, separates 5, counts remaining cubes
Problem #9 Nonroutine Correct: no	Strategy: direct model—sets out 7 markers, distributes one at a time to the 7, gets confused in the process and needs help

Name: E (H.G.)
Age: 6 yrs. 3 mo.
Birthdate: 2/18/88
Date: May 18, 1994 (tape C)

Problem #1 SRU Correct: yes	Strategy: direct model—sets out 13 cubes, seperates 7 cubes, counts remaining cubes
Problem #2 JCU Correct: yes	Strategy: direct model—sets out 7 cubes, joins on 4, counts number joined
Problem #3 C Correct: yes	Strategy: direct model—sets out 12 cubes, sets out 7 cubes, matches, counts difference
Problem #4 M Correct: yes	Strategy: direct model—sets out 3 markers, distributes 6 to each of the markers, counts total
Problem #5 MD Correct: yes	Strategy: sets out 15 cubes, separates into groups of 3, counts number of groups of 3
Problem #6 PD Correct: yes	Strategy: direct model—sets out 20 cubes sets out 4 markers, distributes the 20 cubes first 2 at a time and then adjusts, counts number of cubes in each group
Problem #7 D/re Correct: yes	Strategy: direct model—sets out 1 marker at a time and distributes 5 cubes to it, continues until has distributed 4 groups, checks total number of cubes distributed, removes one, counts groups
Problem #8 Multistep Correct: yes	Strategy: direct model—sets out 3 markers, distributes 4 cubes to each, removes 5 cubes, counts remaining cubes
Problem #9 Nonroutine Correct: yes	Strategy: direct model—sets out 19 cubes, divides the cubes into groups of 3 and 2 to make 7 groups, counts number of groups with 3 and with 2

Name: F (W.G.)
Age: 5 yrs. 11 mo.
Birthdate: 6/22/88
Date: May 18, 1994

Problem #1 SRU Correct: yes	Strategy: direct model—draws 13 tallys, erases 6 tallys, counts remaining tallys
Problem #2 JCU Correct: no	Strategy: randomly sets out 5 cubes, starts to distribute 3 cubes to each, becomes confused, does not solve
Problem #3 C Correct: no	Strategy: sets out 7, sets out 12, keeps saying 12 is more. Does not solve.
Problem #4 M Correct: yes	Strategy: direct model—sets out 3 markers, distributes 6, counts all
Problem #5 MD Correct: no	Strategy: not given
Problem #6 PD Correct: no	Strategy: not given
Problem #7 D/re Correct: no	Strategy: not given
Problem #8 Multistep Correct: no	Strategy: not given
Problem #9 Nonroutine Correct: no	Strategy: not given

Name: G (G.H.)
Age: 5 yrs. 9 mo.
Birthdate: 8/17/88
Date: May 18, 1994 (tape B)

Problem #1 SRU Correct: yes	Strategy: direct model—sets out 13, seperates 6, counts remaining cubes
Problem #2 JCU Correct: yes miscount	Strategy: direct model—sets out 7, joins to make 11, counts number of cubes joined
Problem #3 C Correct: yes	Strategy: direct model—sets out 7 cubes, sets out 12 cubes, lines cubes up to match, counts difference
Problem #4 M Correct: yes	Strategy: direct model—sets out 3 markers, distributes 6 to each marker, counts total distributed
Problem #5 MD Correct: yes	Strategy: direct model—links 15 cubes, sets out 10 cubes, breaks off 3 at a time and distributes to markers, removes extra markers, counts number of groups
Problem #6 PD Correct: yes	Strategy: direct model—sets out 20 cubes sets out 4 markers, distributes the 20 cubes one at a time, counts number of cubes in each group
Problem #7 D/re Correct: no	Strategy: direct model—sets out 19 cubes, randomly sets out 6 cubes, distributes the 19 cubes one at a time, becomes confused and pulls all 19 cubes together again, sets out 6 cubes and distributes the 19 cubes 5 at a time, counts number of groups, at first uncertain that one group can have 4 but decides it's okay, solves with help
Problem #8 Multistep Correct: yes	Strategy: direct model—sets out 3 markers, distributes 4 to each of the 3 cubes, seperates 5, counts remaining cubes
Problem #9 Nonroutine Correct: no	Strategy: direct model—sets out 19 cubes , sets out 7 cubes, distributes cubes three at a time to the 7, becomes confused, solves with help

Name: H (J.H.)
Age: 6 yrs. 8 mo.
Birthdate: 9/20/87
Date: May 17, 1994 (tape A2)

Problem #1 SRU Success: yes	Strategy: direct model—sets out 13 cubes, removes 6 cubes, counts remaining cubes
Problem #2 JCU Success: yes	Strategy: direct model—draws 7 tallys, joins on 4 more
Problem #3 C Correct: yes	Strategy: direct model—links 12 cubes, links 7 cubes, matches, counts difference
Problem #4 M Correct: yes	Strategy: direct model—sets out 3 markers, distributes 6 cubes to each of the 3, counts
Problem #5 MD Correct: yes	Strategy: direct model—sets out 5 markers, sets out 15 cubes, removes 2 markers, distributes the 15 cubes to the 3 markers 3 at a time, returns the 2 markers, continues to distribute, counts groups
Problem #6 PD Correct: yes	Strategy: direct model—using slate draws 4 boxes, draws 20 tallys beneath the boxes, disbributes tallys to the boxes one at a time erasing used tallys, counts number of tallys in a box, distributes remainder one at a time, counts number in each group
Problem #7 D/re Correct: yes	Strategy: direct model—sets out 3 markers, sets out 19 cubes, counts cubes, distributes the 19 cubes 5 at a time, adds one more marker, counts number of groups, it's okay for one group to have 4
Problem #8 Multistep Correct: yes	Strategy: direct model—sets out 3 markers, distributes 4 cubes to each of the 3, seperates 5, counts the remaining cubes
Problem #9 Nonroutine Correct: yes	Strategy: direct model—sets out 7 markers, sets out 19 cubes, distributes the cubes 3 at a time, adjusts so 2 groups have 2 cubes, counts

Name: I (M.K.)
Age: 6 yrs. 1 mo.
Birthdate: 4/25/88
Date: May 12, 1994 (tape A1)

Problem #1 SRU Correct: yes	Strategy: direct model—sets out 13 cubes, removes 6, counts remaining cubes
Problem #2 JCU Correct: no	Strategy: sets out 7, sets out 11, counts both groups together
Problem #3 C Correct: no	Strategy: sets out 12, sets out 7, keeps saying there are 12 more
Problem #4 M Correct: no	Strategy: sets out 3 cubes, sets out 6, counts both sets together
Problem #5 MD Correct: no	Strategy: sets out 3, sets out 15, joins both sets together
Problem #6 PD Correct: yes	Strategy: direct model—sets out 20 cubes sets out 4 cubes, distributes the 20 cubes 4 at a time, then one at a time, , counts number within groups
Problem #7 D/re Correct: no	Strategy: direct model—sets out 19 cubes, separates into groups of 5 and 4, it's all right if one group has 4 cubes, counts groups, solves with help
Problem #8 Multistep Correct: no	Strategy: direct model—sets out 3 markers, sets out 4, gets confused, solves with help
Problem #9 Nonroutine Correct: no	Strategy: not given

Name: J (L.J.)
Age: 6 yrs. 2 mo.
Birthdate: 3/23/87
Date: May 17, 1994

Problem #1 SRU Correct: yes	Strategy: direct model—sets out 13 cubes, seperates 7, counts remaining cubes
Problem #2 JCU Correct: no	Strategy: sets out 7, sets out 11, joins all
Problem #3 C Correct: no	Strategy: sets out 12, sets out 7, states that 12 is more
Problem #4 M Correct: yes	Strategy: direct model—sets out 3 cubes, distributes 6 cubes to each of the three, counts total
Problem #5 MD Correct: no	Strategy: direct model—sets out 15 cubes, randomly sets out 4 cubes, distributes 3 cubes to each of the 4 cubes, adds another cube and distributes 3 more, counts number of groups with 3, solves with help
Problem #6 PD Correct: yes	Strategy: direct model—sets out 20 cubes, sets out 4 markers, distributes the 20 cubes 1 at a time to the 4, counts number in each group
Problem #7 D/re Correct: no	Strategy: did not give
Problem #8 Multistep Correct: yes	Strategy: direct model—sets out 3 cubes, distributes 4 cubes to each of the 3, removes 5, counts remaining cubes
Problem #9 Nonroutine Correct: no	Strategy: did not give

Name: K (A.M.)
Age: 6 yrs. 2 mo.
Birthdate: 3/24/88
Date: May 17, 1994 (tape B)

Problem #1 SRU Correct: yes	Strategy: direct model—sets out 13, seperates 6, counts remaining cubes
Problem #2 JCU Correct: yes	Strategy: direct model—sets out 7, joins on 4, counts number joined
Problem #3 C Correct: yes	Strategy: direct model—sets out 12, sets out 7, matches, counts difference
Problem #4 M Correct: yes	Strategy: direct model—sets out 3 cubes, distributes 6 to each cube, counts distributed cubes
Problem #5 MD Correct: yes	Strategy: direct model—sets out 15, randomly sets out 5 cubes, distributes 3 to each of the 5, counts number of cubes that had randomly set out
Problem #6 PD Correct: no	Strategy: sets out 20, sets out 4, distributes 4 at a time to each of the 4 cubes, distributes the remainder one at a time, counts, solves with help
Problem #7 D/re Correct: yes	Strategy: direct model—sets out 19, randomly sets out 5, distributes 5 to each cube from the 19, counts and checks there were 19, pushes extra cube away, counts, it's okay to have one group of 4
Problem #8 Multistep Correct: yes	Strategy: direct model—sets out 4 cubes, distributes 4 to each cube, seperates 5, counts remaining cubes
Problem #9 Nonroutine Correct: yes	Strategy: direct model—sets out 19, sets out 7 markers, distributes 3 at a time to each of the 7, adjusts the single cube by taking from a group of 3

Name: L (M.P.)
Age: 5 yrs. 9 mo.
Birthdate: 8/29/88
Date: May 19, 1994 (tape C)

Problem #1 SRU Correct: yes	Strategy: direct model—sets out 13 cubes, seperates 6, counts remaining cubes
Problem #2 JCU Correct: yes	Strategy: direct model—sets out 11 cubes, recounts the 11, pauses after saying "7", continues to count, and says "4"
Problem #3 C Correct: yes m	Strategy: direct model—lines up 12 cubes, lines up 7 cubes, matches, counts difference
Problem #4 M Correct: yes	Strategy: direct model—sets out 3 markers, distributes 6 cubes to each of the 3, counts the cubes all together
Problem #5 MD Correct: yes	Strategy: direct model—sets out 15 cubes, sets out 7 markers, distributes 3 cubes to the 7 cubes, removes extra markers, counts number of groups
Problem #6 PD Correct: no	Strategy: direct model—sets out 20 cubes, sets out 4 markers, distributes the cubes first 3 at a time to the 4, continues distributing remaining cubes, keeps adjusting numbers in each group, becomes confused, solves with help
Problem #7 D/re Correct: yes	Strategy: direct model—sets out 19 cubes, randomly sets out 6 markers, distributes the cubes 5 at a time until one cube is given only 4, removes extra markers, groups of 5 are counted, okay for one group to have 4
Problem #8 Multistep Correct: yes	Strategy: direct model—sets out 3 cubes, distributes 4 cubes to each of the first 3 cubes, removes 5, counts remaining cubes
Problem #9 Nonroutine Correct: yes	Strategy: direct model—sets out a row of 19 cubes, sets out 7 cubes next to the 19, distributes the 19 cubes in groups of 3 and then in groups of 2, counts groups

Name: M (E.S.)
Age: 6 yrs. 5 mo.
Birthdate: 12/30/87
Date: May 17, 1994

Problem #1 SRU Correct: yes miscount	Strategy: direct model—sets out 13 cubes, separates 6 cubes, counts remaining cubes
Problem #2 JCU Correct: yes miscount	Strategy: counts—says, “eight, nine, ten, eleven. Four.” First attempt miscounts in head
Problem #3 C Correct: yes	Strategy: direct model—sets out 12 cubes, sets out 7 cubes, matches, counts difference
Problem #4 M Correct: yes miscount	Strategy: direct model—sets out 3 markers, distributes 6 cubes to each of the 3, counts
Problem #5 MD Correct: yes	Strategy: direct model—sets out 15 cubes, separates the 15 into groups of 3, counts number of groups
Problem #6 PD Correct: yes miscount	Strategy: direct model—sets out 20 cubes, separates the 20 cubes into 4 groups and adjusts to get the same number in each group , counts number in each group
Problem #7 D/re Correct: yes	Strategy: direct model—sets out 20, changes to 19, lines up into groups of 5, counts number of groups, its okay to have one group to have 4
Problem #8 Multistep Correct: yes	Strategy: direct model—sets out 3 groups of 4, separates 5 cubes, counts remaining cubes
Problem #9 Nonroutine Correct: yes	Strategy: direct model—sets out 19 cubes, separates the 19 cubes into groups of 3, separates last cubes into groups with 2, counts

Name: N (P.S.)
Age: 6 yrs.
Birthdate: 5/29/88
Date: May 12, 1994 (tape A1)

Problem #1 SRU Correct: yes	Strategy: direct model—sets out 13 cubes, removes 6 cubes, counts remaining cubes
Problem #2 JCU Correct: yes	Strategy: direct model—sets out 7 cubes, counts while joining to 11, says "4"
Problem #3 C Correct: yes	Strategy: direct model—sets out 12 cubes, sets out 7 cubes, matches, counts difference
Problem #4 M Correct: yes	Strategy: direct model—sets out 3 markers, distributes 6 cubes to each of the 3, counts total
Problem #5 MD Correct: yes	Strategy: direct model—sets out 15 cubes, sets out 3 markers, distributes 3 cubes to each of the 3, splits remaining into wo groups of 3 without having to use additional markers, counts groups
Problem #6 PD Correct: yes	Strategy: direct model—sets out 4 markers, sets out 20, distributes the 20 one at a time to the 4 cubes , counts total in each group
Problem #7 D/re Correct: yes	Strategy: direct model—sets out 19 cubes, separates into 3 groups of 5 and one group of 4, counts groups, it's okay to have one group of 4
Problem #8 Multistep Correct: yes	Strategy: direct model—sets out 3 markers, distributes 4 cubes to each of the 3, removes 5, counts remaining cubes
Problem #9 Nonroutine Correct: yes	Strategy: direct model—sets out 19, separates into groups of 3 and 2, counts groups

Name: O (I.S.)
Age: 6 yrs. 6 mo.
Birthdate: 11/24/87
Date: May 12, 1994 (tape A1)

Problem #1 SRU Correct: yes	Strategy: direct model—sets out 13 cubes, removes 6 cubes, counts remaining cubes
Problem #2 JCU Correct: yes	Strategy: counts—uses fingers and says "8, 9, 10, 11. It's 4."
Problem #3 C Correct: yes	Strategy: direct model—sets out 12 cubes, sets out 7 cubes, matches, counts difference
Problem #4 M Correct: yes	Strategy: direct model—sets out 3 markers, distributes 6 cubes to each of the 3, counts
Problem #5 MD Correct: yes	Strategy: direct model—sets out 15 cubes, sets out 3 markers, distributes 3 cubes to each of the 3, adds cubes and distributes remaining cubes, counts groups
Problem #6 PD Correct: yes	Strategy: direct model—sets out 20 cubes, sets out 4 markers, distributes the 20 cubes first 4 at a timeand then one at a time to the 4 , counts number of cubes in each group
Problem #7 D/re Correct: yes	Strategy: direct model—sets out 3 markers, distributes 4 cubes to each of the 3, removes 5, counts remaining cubes
Problem #8 Multistep Correct: yes	Strategy: direct model—ets out 3 markers, distributes 4 to each of the 3, separates 5, counts remaining cubes
Problem #9 Nonroutine Correct: yes	Strategy: direct model—sets out 19 cubes, sets out 7 markers, distributes the 19 first 2 at a time then adds the remaining to have groups with 3, counts groups with 2 and groups with 3

Name: P (F.T.)
Age: 6 yrs. 4 mo.
Birthdate: 1/6/88
Date: May 17, 1994 (tape A2)

Problem #1 SRU Correct: yes	Strategy: direct model—sets out 13 cubes, separates 6 bues, counts remaining cubes
Problem #2 JCU Correct: yes *** (uses matching)	Strategy: direct model—sets out 7 cubes, sets out 11 cubes, matches, counts difference to find 4 more
Problem #3 C Correct: yes	Strategy: direct model—lines up 12 cubes, lines up 7 cubes, matches, counts difference
Problem #4 M Correct: yes	Strategy: direct model—sets out 3 markers, distributes 6 cubes to each of the three, counts all
Problem #5 MD Correct: yes	Strategy: direct model—sets out 15 cubes, and 8 markers, distributes the 15 to the 8, removes extra markers, counts groups of 3
Problem #6 PD Correct: yes	Strategy: direct model—sets out 20 cubes, sets out 4 markers, distributes the 20 cubes to the 4 markerss 4 at a time, the remaining cubes are distributed one at a time, counts number in each group
Problem #7 D/re Correct: yes	Strategy: direct model—sets out 19 cubes, sets out 10 markers, distributes the 19 cubes to the 10 markers 5 at a time, removes extra markers, counts number of groups, explains one group will have 4
Problem #8 Multistep Correct: yes	Strategy: direct model—sets out 3 markers, distributes 4 cubes to each of the 3, removes 5 cubes, counts remaining cubes
Problem #9 Nonroutine Correct: yes	Strategy: direct model—sets out 19 cubes, lines up 7 markers, distributes the 19 cubes to the 7 markers 3 cubes at a time, gets confused, starts over, sets out 19 cubes, lines up 7, distributes the cubes 3 at a time to the 7, puts 2 cubes in last two, counts groups

Name: Q (L.W.)
Age: 6 yrs. 2 mo.
Birthdate: 3/17/88
Date: May 12, 1994 (tape A1)

Problem #1 SRU Correct: yes	Strategy: direct model—sets out 13 cubes, removes 6 cubes, counts remaining cubes
Problem #2 JCU Correct: yes	Strategy: direct model—sets out 7 cubes, joins 4 cubes, counts number added
Problem #3 C Correct: yes	Strategy: direct model—sets out 12 cubes, sets out 7 cubes, matches, counts difference
Problem #4 M Correct: yes	Strategy: direct model—sets out 3 markers, distributes 3 cubes to each of the 3, counts
Problem #5 MD Correct: yes	Strategy: direct model—sets out 5 markers, distributes 3 cubes to each of the 5, counts total distributed cubes, counts total groups
Problem #6 PD Correct: yes	Strategy: direct model—sets out 20 cubes sets out 4 markers, distributes the 20 cubes 4 at a time to each of the 4, distributes the remaining cubes one at a time, counts number of cubes in each group
Problem #7 D/re Correct: yes	Strategy: direct model—sets out 19 cubes, sets out 4 markers, distributes 5 cubes to ach of the 4, recounts, removes extra cube, counts number of groups, it's okay for one group to have 4
Problem #8 Multistep Correct: yes	Strategy: direct model—sets out 3 markers, distributes 4 cubes to each of the 3, removes 5, counts remaining cubes
Problem #9 Nonroutine Correct: no	Strategy: direct model—sets out 8 markers, (one extra cube for driver), sets out 19 cubes, distributes cubes to each of the seven, keeps adjusting number of cubes within groups until 19 has been distributed, counts number of groups with 2 cubes, solves with help

Bibliography

Allison, J., & Spence, M. 1993. *A story of contradiction and contrast: A case study of a "reformed" mathematics classroom.* Unpublished paper. Madison: University of Wisconsin.

Au, K., & Jordon, C. 1981. Teaching reading to Hawaiian children: Finding a culturally appropriate solution. In H. Trueba, G. Guthrie, & K. Au (Eds.), *Culture and the bilingual classroom: Studies in classroom ethnography* 139–152. Rowlet, MA: Newbury House.

Banks, J. 1988. *Multiethnic education: Theory and practice* 2d ed. Boston, MA: Allyn & Bacon, Inc.

Basso, K. 1970. To give up on words: Silence in Western Apache culture. *Southwestern Journal of Anthropology* 26: 213–130.

Brassard, M. R., & Szaraniec, L. 1983. Promoting early school achievement in American Indian children. *School Psychology International* 4: 91–100.

Bourdieu, P. 1991. Language and Symbolic Power. Cambridge, MA: Harvard University Press.

Butterfield, A. 1983. The development and use of culturally appropriate curriculum for American Indian students. *Peabody Journal of Education* 61: 50–66.

Butterfield, R. A. 1985. *Effective practices in Indian education: A monograph for using and developing culturally appropriate curriculum for American Indian students.* Portland, OR: Northwest Regional Educational Laboratory.

Cajete, G. A. 1988. *Motivating American Indian students in science and math.* Las Cruces, NM: ERIC Clearing House on Rural Education and Small Schools.

Cahape, P., & Howley, C. B. (Eds.). 1992. *Indian nations at risk: Listening to the people.* Charleston, WV: Appalachia Educational Laboratiry, ERIC Clearing House on Rural Education and Small Schools.

Carey, D. A., Fennema, E., Carpenter, T. P., & Franke, M. L. 1994. Cognitively Guided Instruction: Towards Equitable Classrooms. In W. Secada, E. Fennema, & L. Byrd (Eds.). *New directions in equity for mathematics education.* New York: Teachers College Press.

Carpenter, T. P. 1985. Learning to add and subtract: An exercize in problem solving. In E. A. Silver (Ed.), *Teaching and learning mathematical problem solving: Multiple research perspectives* 17–40. Hillsdale, NJ: Lawrence Erlbaum.

Carpenter, T. P., Ansell, E., Franke, M., Fennema, E., & Weisbeck, L. 1993. Models of problem solving: A study of kindergarten children's problem-solving processes. *Journal for Research in Mathematics Education* 24(5): 427–440.

Carpenter, T. P., & Fennema, E. 1992. Cognitively guided instruction: Building on the knowledge of students and teachers. In W. Secada (Ed.), *Curriculum reform: The case of mathematics in the United States*. Special issue of the *International Journal of Educational Research* 457–470. Elmswood, NY: Pergamon Press, Inc.

Cazden, C. 1988. *Classroom discourse: The language of teaching and learning*. Portsmouth, NH: Heinemann Educational Books.

Cheek, H. 1983. *Proposal to develop culturally based programs in mathematics*. Stillwater, OK.

Cocking, R. R., & Chipman, S. 1988. Conceptual issues related to mathematics achievement of language minority children. In R. R. Cocking & J. P Mestre (Eds.), *Linguistics and cultural influences on learning mathematics*. Hillsdale, NJ: Lawrence.

Erickson, F., & Mohatt, G. 1982. Cultural organization of the participation structures in two classrooms of Indian students. In G. Spindler (Ed.), *Doing the ethnography of schooling* 131–174. NY: Holt, Rinehart & Winston.

Eriks-Brophy, A, & Crago, M. B. 1993. *Transforming classroom discourse: Forms of evaluation in Inuit IR and IRe routines*. Paper presented at the American Educational Research Convention, Atlanta, GA.

Ernest, P. 1991. *The philosophy of mathematics education*. New York: Palmer Press.

Fairclough, N. 1989. *Language and power*. London: Longman.

Fedullo, M. 1992. *A teacher's journey into Native American classrooms and culture*. New York: Anchor Books, Doubleday.

Fennema, E., Carpenter, T. A., & Peterson, P. L. 1989. Teachers' decision making and cognitively guided instruction: A new paradigm for curriculum development. In N. F. Ellerton & M. A. Clements (Eds.), *School mathematics: The challenge to change* 174–187. Geelong, Victoria, Australia: Deakin University press.

Fennema, E., Carpenter, T., Franke, M., Levi, L., Jacobs, V., and Empson, S. 1994. *Mathematics instruction and teacher's beliefs: A longitudinal study of using children's thinking*. (Submitted for publication).

Fletcher, J. D. 1983. *What problems do American Indians have with mathematics?* Provo, UT.

Fosnot, C. T. 1989. *Enquiring teachers, enquiring learners: A constructivist approach for teaching*. New York: Teachers College Press.

Foster, S. 1989. *Out of school mathematics teaching: Content and instruction as reported by Bad River Anishinabeg.* Unpublished Master's Thesis, Madison: University of Wisconsin.

Foucault, M. 1972. *The archaeology of knowledge and the discourse on language.* Trans. A. M. Sheridan Smith. New York: Pantheon Books.

Freudenthal, H. 1991. *Revisiting mathematics education: China lectures.* Dordrecht: Kluwer Academic Publishers.

Fries, J. E. 1987. *The American Indian in higher education: 1975–1976 to 1984–1985.* Washington DC: US Government Printing Office.

Fuchs, E., & Havighurst, R. J. 1973. *To live on this earth: American Indian education.* New York: Anchor Press, Doubleday.

Fuson, K. C. 1992. Research on whole number additiona and subtraction. In D. Grouws (Ed.), *Handbook of research on mathematics teaching and learning* 243–275. New York: McMillan.

Gardner, H. 1985. *The mind's new science: A history of the cognitive revolution.* New York: Basic Books.

Gee, J. P. 1986. Units in the production of narrative discourse. *Discourse Processes* 9: 391–422.

Gergen, K. 1985. Social constructionist inquiry: Context and implications. In K. Gergen & K. Davis (Eds.), *The social construction of the person* 3–18. New York: Springer-Verlag.

Ghaleb, M. S. 1992. *Performance and solution strategies of Arabic-speaking second graders in simple addition and subtraction word problems and relation of their performance to their degree of bilingualism.* Unpublished dissertation. Madison: University of Wisconsin.

Gilliland, H. 1992. *Teaching the Native American* 2d ed. Dubuque: Kendal Hunt.

Gollnick, G. 1993. Comments made by Genny Gollnick, curriculum coordinator of the Oneida Tribal School, during a conversation about storytelling.

Good, T. L., & Brophy, J. 1987. *Looking in classrooms.* London: Harper & Row Publishers.

Goodenough, W. 1971. *Culture, language, and society.* Addison- Wesley module. Reading, MA: Addison-Wesley Publishing Company.

Green, R. 1978. Math avoidance: A barrier to American Indian science education and science careers. *BIA Education Research Bulletin* 6(3): 1–8.

Green, R., Brown, J. W., & Long, R. 1978. *Report and recommendations: Conference on mathematics in American Indian education.* Washington, DC: Educational Foundation of America and American Association for the Advancement of Science.

Greenbaum, P. 1983. *Nonverbal communications between American Indian children and their teachers.* Lawrence, KS: Native American Research Associates. (ERIC Document Reproduction Service No. ED 239 804).

Greer, B. 1992. Multiplication and division as models of situations. In D. Grouws (Ed.), *Handbook of research on mathematics teaching and learning* 276–295. New York: McMillan.

Guilmet, G. M. 1979. Maternal perceptions of urban Navajo and Caucasion children's classroom behavior. *Human Organization* 38: 87–91.

Hadfield, O. D. 1982. Mathematics anxiety and learning style of the Navajo middle school student. *School Science and Mathematics* 92(4): 172–760.

Hallowell, A. I. 1955. *Culture and experience*. Philadelphia: University of Pennsylvania Press.

Hillabrant, W., Romano, M., Stang, D. & Charleston, M. 1992. Native American education at a turning point: Current deomgraphics and trends [Summary]. In P. Cahape & C. B. Howley (Eds.), *Indian nations at risk: Listening to the people* 6–9. Charleston, WV: ERIC Clearing House on Rural Education and Small Schools.

Indian Nations at Risk Task Force. 1992. *Indian Nations at Risk: An Educational Strategy for Action*. Washington, DC: Department of Education.

Johnson, M. L. 1982. *Blacks in mathematics: The state of the art*. Paper presented at the NCTM Equity in Mathematics Core Conference, Reston, VA.

Jordan, C. 1985. Translating culture: From ethnographic information to educational program. Anthropology and Education Quarterly 16: 105–123.

Jordan, C., Tharpe, R. G. 1979. Culture and Education. In A. J. Marsella, R. G. Tharpe, & T. Ciborowski (Eds.), *Perspectives in cross-cultural psychology*. New York: Academic.

Kinietz, W. V. 1972. *The Indians of the western great lakes: 1615–1760*. Ann Arbor: University of Michigan Press (1st ed., 1940).

Kouba, V. 1989. Children's solution strategies for equivalent set multiplication and division word problems. *Journal for Research in Mathematics Education* 20: 147–158.

Ladson-Billings, G. (in press). Toward a theory of relevant pedagogy. *Educational Research Journal*.

Lane, M. 1988. *Women and minorities in science and engineering*. Washington DC: National Science Foundation.

Leap, W. L. 1988. Assumptions and strategies guiding mathematics problem-solving by Ute students. In R. Cocking, R. and J. Mestre (Eds.), *Linguistic and cultural experiences on learning mathematics*. Hillsdale, NJ: Lawrence Erlbaum Associates.

Leavitt, R. M. 1983. Storytelling as language curriculum. In W. Carsen (Ed.), *Actes du quartorzieme Congres de Algonquistes* 27–33.

Lipka, J. 1991. Toward a culturally based pedagogy: A case study of one Yup'ik Eskimo teacher. *Anthropology and Education Quarterly* 22: 203–223.

Lombardi, T. P. 1970. Psycholinguistic abilities of Papago Indian children. *Exceptional Children* 36: 485–493.

McDermott, R. P. 1976. *Kids make sense: An ethnographic account of the interactional management of success and failure in one first-grade classroom.* Unpublished dissertation. Stanford University, Anthropology Department.

Macias, C. J. 1989. American Indian academic success: The role of indigenous learning strategies. *Journal of American Indian Education* 28: 43–51.

Mohatt, G., & Erickson, F. 1981. Cultural differences of teaching styles in an Odawa School: A sociolinguistic approach. In H. Trueba, G. Guthrie, & K. Au (Eds.), *Culture and the bilingual classroom: Studies in classroom ethnography* 105–119. Rowley, MA: Newbury House.

Narayan, K. 1993. How native is a "native" anthropologist? *American Anthropologist* 95: 671–686.

Nash, R. 1973. *Classrooms observed: The teacher's perceptions and the pupil's performance.* Boston: Routledge & Kegan Paul.

National Council of Teachers of Mathematics. 1989. *Curriculum and evaluation standards for school mathematics.* Reston, VA: Author.

National Council of Teachers of Mathematics. 1991. *Teaching standards for school mathematics.* Reston, VA: Author.

National Research Council. 1990. *Reshaping school mathematics: A philosophy and framework for curriculum.* Washington, DC: National Academy Press.

Ortiz-Franco, L. 1981. *Suggestions for increasing the participation of minorities in scientific research.* Washington, DC: National Institute of Education.

Patton, M. Q. 1975. *Alternative evaluation paradigm.* Grand Forks, ND: University of North Dakota Press.

Philips, Susan U. 1983. *The invisible culture: Communication in classroom and community on the Warm Springs Indian Reservation.* New York, NY: Longman Inc.

Popkewitz, T.P. 1991. *A Political Sociology of Educational Reform.* New. York, New York: Teachers College Press.

Preston, V. 1991. *Mathematics and science curricula in elementary and secondary education for American Indian and Alaska Native students.* In Indian nations at risk task force commissioned papers.

Resnick, L. B. 1987. *Education and learning to think.* Washington, DC: National Academy Press.

Rhodes, R. W. 1989. Native American leaning Styles. *Journal of Navajo Education* 7: 33–41.

Romberg, T. A. 1992. Problematic features of the school mathematics curriculum. In P. Jackson (Ed.), *Handbook of research on curriculum.* New York: Mcmillan.

Romberg, T. A., & Carpenter, T. P. 1986. Research on teaching and learning mathematics: Two disciplines of scientific inquiry. In M.

Wittrock (Ed.), *The third handbook of research on teaching*. New York: Mcmillan.
Ross, A. C. 1989. Brain hemispheric functions and the Native American. *Journal of American Indian Education* 28: 72–75.
Stuck in the horizon: A special report on the education of Native Americans 1989, April 2. *Education Week* 1–16.
Vernaud, G. 1983. Multiplicative Structures. In R. Lesh & M. Landau (Eds.), *Acquisition of mathematical concepts and processes* 127–174. New York: Acadmic Press.
Vogt, L., Jordon, C., & Tharp, R. 1987. Explaining school failure, producing school success: Two cases. *Anthropology and Education Qurterly* 18: 276–286.
Scollon, R., & Scollon S. K. 1981. *Narrative, literacy, and face in interethnic communication*. Norwood, NJ: Ablex.
Scott, P. B. 1983. Mathematics achievement test scores of American Indian and Anglo students: A comparison. *Journal of American Indian Education* 22(3): 17–19.
Shotter, J. 1993. *Culture politics of everyday life: Social constructionism, rhetoric, and knowing of the third kind.* Toronto: University of Toronto Press.
Silliman, E., & Wilkinson, L. C. 1991. *Communicating for learning: Classroom observation and collaboration*. Gaithersberg, MD: Aspen.
Smith, H. A. 1988. *Abduction and the signs of expertise*. Paper presented at the annual meeting of the American Educational Research Association, New Orleans, LA.
Spanos, G. et al. 1988. Linguistic features of mathematical problem solving: Insights and applications. In R. Cocking & J. Mestre (Eds.), *Linguistic and cultural influences on learning mathematics*. Hillsdale, NJ: Lauwrence Erlbaum and Associates.
Spindler, G., & Spindler, L. 1971. *Dreamers without power: The Menomini*. New York: Holt, Rineholt and Winston.
Spradely, J. 1979. *The ethnographic interview*. New York: Holt, Rinehart, & Winston.
Swisher, K., & Deyhle, D. 1989. The styles of learning are different but the teaching is just the same: Suggestions for teachers of American Indian youth. *Journal of American Indian Education* 28: 1–13.
Tafoya, T. 1982. Coyote's eyes: Native cognition styles. *Journal of American Indian Education* 21: 21–33.
Tharp, R. G. 1994. Intergroup differences among Native Americans in socialization and child cognition: An ethnogenetic analysis. In P. Greenfiled & R. Cocking (Eds.), *Cross-cultural roots of minority child development* 87–105. Hillsdale, NJ: Erlbaum.
Tharp, R. G. , & Yamauchi, L. A. 1994. *Effective instructional conversation in native American classrooms*. A report prepared for the National Center for Research on Cultural Diversity and Second Language Learning, University of California, Santa Cruz.